Blacks in Film

Lucent Library of Black History

William W. Lace

LUCENT BOOKS

A part of Gale, Cengage Learning

GALE
CENGAGE Learning

Detroit • New York • San Francisco • New Haven, Conn • Waterville, Maine • London

GALE
CENGAGE Learning™

LIBRARY OF CONGRESS CATALOGING-IN-PUBLICATION DATA

Lace, William W.
  Blacks in film / by William W. Lace.
    p. cm. — (Lucent library of Black history)
  Includes bibliographical references and index.
  ISBN 978-1-4205-0084-4 (hbk.)
  1. African Americans in motion pictures—Juvenile literature. 2. African Americans in the motion picture industry—Juvenile literature. I. Title.
  PN1995.9.N4L33 2008
    791.43089'96073—dc22

                                                        2008018289

Lucent Books
27500 Drake Rd.
Farmington Hills, MI 48331

ISBN-13: 978-1-4205-0084-4
ISBN-10: 1-4205-0084-8

Contents

Foreword

It has been more than 500 years since Africans were first brought to the New World in shackles, and over 140 years since slavery was formally abolished in the United States. Over 50 years have passed since the fallacy of "separate but equal" was obliterated in the American courts, and some 40 years since the watershed Civil Rights Act of 1965 guaranteed the rights and liberties of all Americans, especially those of color. Over time, these changes have become celebrated landmarks in American history. In the twenty-first century, African American men and women are politicians, judges, diplomats, professors, deans, doctors, artists, athletes, business owners, and home owners. For many, the scars of the past have melted away in the opportunities that have been found in contemporary society. Observers such as Peter N. Kirsanow, who sits on the U.S. Commission of Civil Rights, point to these accomplishments and conclude, "The growing black middle class may be viewed as proof that most of the civil rights battles have been won."

In spite of these legal victories, however, prejudice and inequality have persisted in American society. In 2003, African Americans comprised just 12 percent of the nation's population, yet accounted for 44 percent of its prison inmates and 24 percent of its poor. Racially motivated hate crimes continue to appear on the pages of major newspapers in many American cities. Furthermore, many African Americans still experience either overt or muted racism in their daily lives. A 1996 study undertaken by Professor Nancy Krieger of the Harvard School of Public Health, for example, found that 80 percent of the African American participants reported having experienced racial discrimination in one or more settings, including at work or school, applying for housing and medical care, from the police or in the courts, and on the street or in a public setting.

It is for these reasons that many believe the struggle for racial equality and justice is far from over. These episodes of discrimination threaten to shatter the illusion that America has completely overcome its racist past, causing many black Americans to become increasingly frustrated and confused. Scholar and writer Ellis Cose has described this splintered state in the following way: "I have done everything I was supposed to do. I have stayed out of trouble with the law, gone to the right schools, and worked myself nearly to death. What more do they want? Why in God's name won't they accept me as a full human being?" For Cose and others, the struggle for equality and justice has yet to be fully achieved.

In many subtle yet important ways the traumatic experiences of slavery and segregation continue to inform the way race is discussed and experienced in the twenty-first century. Indeed, it is possible that America will always grapple with the fallout from its distressing past. Ulric Haynes, dean of the Hofstra University School of Business has said, "Perhaps race will always matter, given the historical circumstances under which we came to this country." But studying this past and understanding how it contributes to present-day dialogues about race and history in America is a critical component of contemporary education. To this end, the Lucent Library of Black History offers a thorough look at the experiences that have shaped the black community and the American people as a whole. Annotated bibliographies provide readers with ideas for further research, while fully documented primary and secondary source quotations enhance the text. Each book in the series explores a different episode of black history; together they provide students with a wealth of information as well as launching points for further study and discussion.

Life Imitates Art Imitates Life

If seeing is indeed believing, then much depends on the source of the vision. If a belief is formed not through firsthand experience but through some filtering medium, then the belief is only as accurate as that filtered view. With a medium as powerful and subjective as the motion picture and an experience as misunderstood as black culture, the result has often been a much-distorted view and false beliefs.

This distortion was especially true in the early days of motion pictures. It is difficult to grasp in these days of video streamed over handheld devices just how compelling the "movies" were in the early 1900s. Suddenly people who had seen a polar bear only in still photographs could see one bounding over an icy field, though another thirty years would pass before they could hear it roar, as well.

The problem for blacks throughout much of the twentieth century was that most Americans were as ignorant of black culture as they were of polar bears. Blacks had been overwhelmingly concentrated in the South until the end of the Civil War in 1865. Over the next sixty years, waves of black Americans migrated to urban centers in the Northeast and Midwest, but there were large swaths of the rural Midwest, northern Great Plains, and West whose residents—most of whom had never traveled more than a few miles from home—had never seen a black person.

False Impressions

Consequently, their impressions of blacks were formed by how blacks were shown in motion pictures. It was not a case of art imitating real life, but of art imitating a white notion of black culture, a nostalgic and usually highly inaccurate look back at pre–Civil War slavery. Most Americans mistook these portrayals as reality.

The struggle for black actors and filmmakers thus has been to bring to the screen—either through mainstream Hollywood films or independent productions—black characters who are full-fleshed human beings instead of stereotypes, and black experience as it was actually lived. This struggle has been long and difficult. Only relatively recently have honest, sensitive, and accurate interpretations of black America been widely available.

Glorifying Crime

According to critics that include prominent national black organizations, some black films have replaced old bad stereotypes with new bad stereotypes. Instead of showing blacks in traditional subservient roles, they have glorified the seamier side of ghetto life. They have held up crime, brutality, and immorality to be the norm rather than the exception. Thus, the impression left with audiences is different but just as inaccurate and just as extreme.

The consequences of this portrayal of black America, one of criminals and hustlers in which the only law is survival, are twofold. First, it has given whites yet another set of misconceptions. Second, it has been charged that the glorification of antisocial behavior has led some blacks, primarily youth, to take on in real life the roles they see on the screen. In this way, art has imitated life, even though inaccurately, and led life to imitate art.

The history of blacks in film as actors and as filmmakers has been one of movement from one extreme stereotype to another. The challenge has been and continues to be for black artists to use their talents in such a way that the life they imitate reflects—in an unwarped mirror—a proud, strong, dignified part of Americana.

Chapter One

Silent Stereotypes

At the dawn of the motion picture era in the late 1800s, American blacks were portrayed accurately, largely because filmmakers did not know how to do otherwise. However, as technology developed and racial attitudes hardened, blacks were pigeonholed into stereotypical roles from which they would struggle long and hard to free themselves.

At first motion pictures were such a novelty that audiences would pay to see virtually anything that showed movement, and that was all that filmmakers needed to produce. Cutting and editing were unknown, so there were no plots. Cameras recorded objects in motion just as they appeared, from a chugging locomotive to a tightrope walker.

To the extent that blacks were pictured at all, they were shown in true-to-life pursuits—working at various jobs. One early film featured a troop of black cavalrymen. Such portrayals, if not always flattering, were at least honest.

Eventually the novelty wore off and these short versions of what today would be called documentaries lost much of their appeal. Editing techniques had advanced, however, to the point where it was possible for a film to tell a story. As soon as films began to follow a plot, the stereotyping of blacks began, or rather began anew, since stage productions dating to the end of the Civil War had already tended to portray blacks as stereotypical prewar characters.

The Stereotypes

In early films, blacks were rarely presented as brutal villains. Instead racist attitudes limited black characters to standard stereotypes categorized by film historian Donald Bogle. The "tom," he writes, was "submissive, stoic, generous, selfless, and oh-so-very kind." The "coon" was "amusement object and black buffoon," usually lazy and unreliable. The "mammy" was independent of mind and "usually big, fat, and cantankerous." Finally, the "tragic mulatto" was doomed to be an outcast, as mixed-race ancestry was socially unacceptable.[1]

The tom was most famously depicted in *Uncle Tom's Cabin* (1903), the first of many films based on Harriet Beecher Stowe's

The 1903 silent movie *Uncle Tom's Cabin* was filled with unflattering stereotypes of blacks in the Civil War era.

antislavery novel. Indeed, the term, which most blacks came to view as an insult, was derived from the title character. This fourteen-minute melodrama was full of stereotypes, including the pickaninny (a young slave child, usually depicted as ragged and mischievous), the mammy figure, and the tragic half-black mulatto. These characters were cast in a sympathetic light, however.

Most other films of the time depicting blacks were less serious. Black characters were often the source of humor or the butt of jokes. In *The Masher* (1907), a young white man, rejected by several girls, finally finds his advances returned by a woman who is mysteriously veiled. When he lifts the veil and finds that the woman is black, however, he runs away in horror. The scene was supposed to be comical, but the film nevertheless conveys the clear message—as do virtually all films of the era—that blacks are inherently inferior and that romantic relationships between blacks and whites are to be avoided at all costs.

Few Black Actors

Although there were black roles in the early silent-film days, there were virtually no black actors, except perhaps those hired as extras in a scene showing slaves at work in a field. The major black characters were played by white actors in "blackface," their faces darkened with theatrical greasepaint, burnt cork, or even shoe polish. Not until 1914, when Sam Lucas played Uncle Tom in the novel's third film version, did black roles begin to go to black actors.

By then, however, the portrayal of blacks in film had undergone a change. Blacks were finding a voice and using it to protest second-class treatment in American society. The National Association for the Advancement of Colored People (NAACP) was founded in 1909 and the National Urban League a year later. At the same time the fiftieth anniversary of the start of the Civil War rekindled old racial animosities, particularly in the South.

Parallel to these developments, moviemaking was becoming less a creative experiment and more a profitable business. Filmmakers such as D.W. Griffith, the Warner brothers, Samuel Goldwyn, Adolph Zukor, and Louis B. Mayer had set up shop in Hollywood, and the industry was beginning to form around a few major studios that controlled all aspects of the final product. As

The Blackface Tradition

The practice of actors portraying blacks in blackface originated long before the Civil War, when blacks appeared onstage only rarely in the North and almost never in the South. So when blacks were to be portrayed either in plays or minstrel shows, white actors would use burnt cork or other media to blacken their faces.

The tradition was so strong that it survived the end of slavery. White actors still occupied most of the black roles, but even black actors used burnt cork to make themselves blacker still. When minstrel shows were succeeded by vaudeville—shows with a series of musical or comedy acts —the blackface tradition continued.

It was natural that the stage tradition carried over to motion pictures. It died out only with the advent of sound films when a demand for more realistic black voices ended the practice of whites masquerading as blacks.

Actor Al Jolson (pictured) gained fame for his portrayals of minstrel players. Many entertainers used blackface in the early twentieth century.

profits became increasingly important, producers became more conservative and more willing to cater to the likes and the dislikes of their paying customers.

The "Rastus" Cycle

The result was that black roles became even more one-dimensional and much more negative. Black characters almost ceased to have any virtues or emotions, except in interactions as inferiors to whites. This development was evident in such films as the series featuring a "coon" character named Rastus, a lazy, good-for-nothing chicken thief. Another series centered on a similar character named Sambo.

Even worse, instead of merely poking fun at blacks, filmmakers began casting them as brutes and criminals. As early as 1907, *The Fights of Nations*, which purported to dramatize conflict within various ethnic groups, showed two urban black men slashing at each other with razors in a fight over a woman.

The greatest influence on the portrayal of blacks in films, however, was the producer-director D.W. Griffith. "More than any other director," film historian Thomas Cripps writes, "Griffith gave future moviemakers a model, a cinematic language, and a rich romantic tradition that would define an Afro-American stereotype."[2]

Griffith's View

Griffith, son of a former Confederate army colonel, saw the Old South as a society in which courage, honor, decency, and duty prevailed in contrast to the squalor and social problems of the large cities of the North. Furthermore, to Griffith the Old South was a well-ordered society in which blacks understood and accepted their roles as inferiors and were governed by benevolent whites. He considered it a tragedy that this ideal world had been swept away by the war.

Griffith fell in love with the theater, became an actor, and moved in 1908 to New York City. There, working for the Biograph Company, he produced more than 450 short films within five years. He founded his own company in Hollywood in 1913 and began to expand on his favorite theme, the romantic and tragic Civil War melodrama.

Griffith was not alone. The Civil War was personal to millions of Americans as well as a pivotal event in American history, and a natural subject for motion pictures. Theater screens were awash with stories of families and lovers separated by the conflict and reunited in the end. Griffith's sense of drama and advanced camera techniques, however, set him apart from other filmmakers. In 1915 he released his most ambitious and successful work, and the film that more than any other set the tone for the portrayal of blacks, *The Birth of a Nation*.

Based on a novel by Thomas Dixon, *The Clansman*, the plot revolves around two families—the northern Stonemans and the southern Camerons—before, during, and mostly after the war. The depiction of some blacks as faithful servants, standing by their former masters after emancipation, was standard. What was new was the extent to which the "bad" blacks were shown as little better than beasts. This was the introduction, Bogle writes, of the final stereotype, "the brutal black buck."[3]

The "Buck" Portrayals

In Griffith's film, ignorant blacks in the postwar South, elevated by northern politicians and soldiers to positions of power, rudely elbow whites off the sidewalk, leer at white women, and drink liquor while sitting in the capitol as legislators. A black named Gus attempts to rape the youngest Cameron daughter, who commits suicide rather than submit. Gus is captured and summarily lynched by the newly formed white supremacist group, the Ku Klux Klan. The mulatto lieutenant governor tries to force the Stoneman daughter to marry him, but in the end she and the Camerons, who are hiding in a cabin besieged by black troops, are saved by Klansmen who ride to the rescue.

The Birth of a Nation made a deep impression on audiences. Not only was the story dramatic, but cinematic techniques had never been put to such uses. In addition, it was the longest film yet made, lasting more than three hours. It was accompanied by specially written music, performed in larger venues by a forty-piece orchestra. Word of mouth and a huge advertising campaign ensured full theaters.

The film was hailed as a masterpiece by critics, even though some deplored its treatment of blacks. The most disturbing

The Birth of a Nation Condemned

The Birth of a Nation, D.W. Griffith's epic film about the post–Civil War South, was considered a cinematic masterpiece. Its depiction of blacks, however, was widely condemned and was the target of protests by the National Association for the Advancement of Colored People (NAACP) and other civil rights groups.

The movie was controversial long after its premiere in 1915. In 1929 an English critic, Oswell Blakeston, wrote, "As a spectacle Griffith's production was awe-inspiring and stupendous, but it has done the Negro irreparable harm. And no wonder, since it was taken from a puerile [childish] novel, *The Clansman*, a book written to arouse racial hate by appealing to the basest passions of the semi-literate."

Black historian Lawrence Reddick, in fact, cited *The Birth of a Nation* as one reason for a dramatic increase in membership of the Ku Klux Klan, a racist organization, in the years after its release.

Source: Quoted in Peter Noble, *The Negro in Films*. New York: Arno, 1970, p. 40.

In 1947 NAACP members picket a revival of the controversial 1915 film *The Birth of a Nation*.

consequence for blacks and their white supporters was that many people accepted the portrayal as historically accurate. Even President Woodrow Wilson said, "My only regret is that it is all so terribly true."[4]

Black Protests

Black leaders were outraged and made their voices heard. Educator W.E.B. DuBois, for example, called the film "the cruel slander upon a weak and helpless race." A black newspaper, the *Chicago Defender*, wrote, "The film viciously plays our race up to the public as being one of rapists and murderers. No more vicious and harmful bit of propaganda has ever been put on the screen."[5] The NAACP labored mightily, but with limited success, to make city censor boards cut some offensive segments. Even white liberals were reluctant to support censorship on freedom of speech grounds.

A scene from *The Birth of a Nation* shows Ku Klux Klan members surrounding a terrified black man. The movie glorified white supremacy.

The furor over *The Birth of a Nation* did ensure that there would be no films matching its negative intensity or social impact. The few imitators failed miserably. Studios, distributors, and theater owners were afraid to touch them. Producers went back to showing blacks in comic or entertainment roles, but the damage had been done. The idea of the black male as a violent sexual predator had been firmly planted in the white American consciousness.

Two years after *The Birth of a Nation* controversy, the United States entered World War I and motion pictures took on a new tone, conveying unity of purpose and the setting aside of differences. Blacks were included, as the government commissioned such films as *Our Colored Fighters* in 1918. One of the most sympathetic portrayals of black-white interaction was *The Greatest Thing in Life*, in which a black private and white officer share a war adventure.

The Twenties

This spirit of brotherhood, however, evaporated with the end of the war. The Roaring Twenties had arrived, and audiences did not want solemn films. They wanted laughter and spectacle, and Hollywood was eager to oblige. Movies grew longer and theaters larger and more lavish. With investors watching closely, producers made films for the mass market to fill those large theaters, in many of which blacks were not allowed.

Black actors were welcome in the films themselves, but only in a narrow range of roles. Critic Geraldyn Dismond wrote in 1929 that "the Negro entered the movies through a back door labeled 'Servants' Entrance.'"[6] Indeed blacks in mainstream movies were maids, butlers, shoeshine boys, all subservient to the white characters. Black entertainers, too, danced across the screen, but almost always for the amusement of whites.

One of the few scenarios in which blacks and whites were anywhere near equal was when they were children. Black child actor Ernest "Sunshine Sammy" Morrison, for example, was such a hit playing opposite white comedian Harold Lloyd that he was one of the first youngsters recruited by Hal Roach for the *Our Gang* series, which began in 1922 and allowed black and white children to play and have adventures in a natural setting.

Cast by Color

■

One of the more subtle forms of racism in films has been white filmmakers' tendency to assign the role of villain to darker-skinned actors while reserving the heroic and romantic parts for those with lighter skin. Women, especially, were cast according to color, and the practice began even before blacks began to appear in major roles.

In 1915's *The Birth of a Nation*, for instance, white actresses in blackface played the roles of Lydia and Mammy. Lydia was light-skinned and slim, while Mammy was very dark and overweight. Film historian Donald Bogle writes:

> This tradition of the desexed, overweight, dowdy *dark* black woman continued in films throughout the 1930s and 1940s. . . . A dark black actress was considered for no other role but that of a mammy or an aunt jemima. On the other hand, the part-black woman—the light-skinned Negress—was given a chance at lead parts and was graced with a modicum of sex appeal. The desirable black women who appeared afterwards in movies were the "cinnamon-colored gals" with Caucasian features. The mulatto came closest to the white ideal. Whether conscious or not [*Birth of a Nation* director D.W.] Griffith's division of the black woman into color categories survived in movies the way many set values continue long after they are discredited.

Source: Donald Bogle, *Toms, Coons, Mulattoes, Mammies & Bucks*. New York: Continuum, 2006, p. 15.

Morrison soon outgrew the role, but his place was taken, in turn, by Allen "Farina" Hoskins," Matthew "Stymie" Beard, and Billie "Buckwheat" Thomas. Some film historians consider *Our Gang* a step forward for blacks. Bogle writes that it "was almost as if there was no such thing as race at all."[7] Others are not so sure. Critic Harry Allan Potamkin calls Farina's character "typical of the . . . Negro as clown, clodhopper or scarecrow."[8]

Certainly these were the treatments blacks received in most of the later silent films. D.W. Griffith might have stopped showing blacks as brutes, but he could still make films such as *One Exciting Night* (1922), in which a white actor in blackface plays Romeo

Washington, whose eyes bug out and hair stands on end while in a haunted house and who, writes Bogle, was "pure coon, a racially crude and self-demeaning character."[9]

The Servants

Apart from savages in jungle adventure films, genial servants were about the only roles for blacks in Roaring Twenties Hollywood, but whatever their nature, mainstream movie roles were increasingly available to black actors. More thoughtful black themes were avoided not only because of audience sensibilities, but also because the industry's Production Code, through its well-meaning prohibition of controversial subjects, deterred exploration of racial issues.

With no new black themes to pursue, filmmakers reverted to old ones. The silent era ended with the 1927 remake of *Uncle Tom's Cabin*, and the casting of the title role showed both how little and how much progress had been made since 1903. Acclaimed black stage actor Charles Gilpin was signed for the part but was fired because his portrayal was considered too aggressive. John B. Lowe took on the role, and his rendering, while not as forceful as Gilpin's, was nevertheless different enough that critic Edith Isaacs could write that his Uncle Tom "seems to wear his ball and chain with a difference."[10]

Later that year the first major sound film, *The Jazz Singer*, was released. The "talkies" gave audiences a taste for realism that would spell the end of blackface and pave the way for Hollywood's first black stars. But it was somehow ironic that *The Jazz Singer* featured a white actor, Al Jolson, in blackface singing a song titled "Mammy."

Chapter Two

The "Race Movies"

"There ought to be serious Negro films since there are Negro novels and plays and poems," British critic Robert Herring wrote in 1927. "There ought to be because here is a race which has, in a short time, expressed itself vitally in literature and the consideration of that literature shows that the qualities which make it so vital are exactly those which films demand."[11]

Some serious films about blacks were made during the silent era. Most filmmakers, however, were content merely to copy white films using black actors. A handful of black filmmakers tried to depict genuine themes, but all were hobbled by low budgets and cutthroat competition from both whites and blacks.

The first known film made specifically for black audiences—films that came to be known as "race movies"—was *The Pullman Porter*, a slapstick comedy made in 1912. However, it was not until 1915 that black intellectuals and civil rights organizations began calling for a film that would counter the negative image made by *The Birth of a Nation*.

The NAACP got Universal Studios to commit $60,000 toward such a film, *Lincoln's Dream*, provided a matching amount could be raised. The NAACP was unable to secure such funding from

The Black Experience

Ossie Davis, the distinguished black actor who appeared in more than forty films and directed *Cotton Comes to Harlem* in 1970, died in 2005 at the age of eighty-five. He was old enough to remember having seen "race movies" in the 1920s and 1930s and recalled the experience:

> There were black people behind the scenes, telling our black story to us as we sat in black theaters. We listened blackly, and a beautiful thing happened to us as we saw ourselves on the screen. We knew that sometimes it was awkward, that sometimes the films behaved differently than the ones we saw in the white theater. It didn't matter. It was ours, and even the mistakes were ours, the fools were ours, the villains were ours, the people who won were ours, and the losers were ours. We were comforted by that knowledge as we sat, knowing that there was something about us up there on that screen, controlled by us, created by us—our own image, as we saw ourselves.

Source: Quoted in William Jones, *Black Cinema Treasures: Lost and Found.* Denton: University of North Texas Press, 1991, p. 6.

Acclaimed actor Ossie Davis, shown here in 1991, was influenced by "race movies" in his early life. Davis had a long, fruitful career.

private investors, however, and when the organization declined to use its own money the project was abandoned.

The Washington Project

Meanwhile black educator Booker T. Washington and his personal secretary, Emmett J. Scott, began looking for ways to form a black-controlled film consortium. One of their ideas was to bring Washington's autobiography *Up from Slavery* to the screen. Such an undertaking, Scott wrote, would show "not only Dr. Washington's personal strivings, but also the strivings of the race climbing up from the tragic period represented by slavery."[12]

The project had not yet begun when Washington died and many investors lost interest. Scott, however, had once been approached about participating in the filming of *Lincoln's Dream*. He resurrected that project, signed a contract with a film company in Chicago owned by Edwin L. Barker, and set about seeking more investors.

However, the contract for *Lincoln's Dream*, which would be retitled *Birth of a Race*, allowed Barker to sell his interest to William Selig, a black filmmaker in Los Angeles. Scott had some success raising money, but when the film was only half finished after two years, Selig backed out and the project was taken over by a Chicago stockbroker who was later arrested for fraudulent stock sales.

Birth of a Race was finally completed, but it bore almost no resemblance to Washington, Scott, and the NAACP's original vision. A long biblical prologue from Adam and Eve through Noah was added, but it had little to do with film footage already shot. Eventually much of the footage featuring blacks was eliminated and the film was turned into a World War I propaganda piece. It premiered in 1918 and was a complete failure. *Variety* magazine called it "the most grotesque cinema chimera [a mythological monster comprising parts of different animals] in the history of the motion picture business."[13]

The Johnson Brothers

George P. Johnson, a postal worker in Omaha, Nebraska, had watched these failures carefully. Johnson and his brother Noble, a black actor who appeared frequently in Universal Studios films, had formed the Lincoln Motion Picture Company in 1916. The Johnsons were convinced that a growing black urban market would support their films. George Johnson wrote that he would "picture the Negro as he is in his every day life, a human being with human inclination, and one of talent and intellect."[14]

George Johnson was determined that his company would avoid the mistakes of others, namely a dependence on white investors,

Urban blacks flock to the movies in 1940. Blacks were happy to see themselves portrayed as real people in "race movies," a change from earlier films.

studios, and distributors. He set up his own network, making contacts with black journalists, distributors, and theater owners throughout the country.

The company's first film, released in 1916, was *The Realization of a Negro's Ambition*, a "two-reeler" running about twenty-five minutes. It starred Noble Johnson as a young man whose persistence and hard work eventually make him wealthy and enable him to marry his boss's daughter. The film was a success with both critics and audiences. Emmett Scott, at the time trying to raise money for *Lincoln's Dream*, invited George Johnson to show it at a meeting of black business leaders whom he was courting.

The Realization of a Negro's Ambition made money, but not enough to finance Lincoln's next film. But between what George could raise and what Noble earned at Universal, they were able to make a second film, *The Trooper of Troop K*. Noble Johnson again played the lead role, a shiftless young man who cannot keep a job and who, at the urging of his sweetheart, joins the army. There he gets a new attitude, distinguishes himself in battle, and eventually returns home to marry his sweetheart.

Financial Challenges

The Trooper of Troop K was even more successful than the Johnsons' first film. It played to a solid week of sold-out urban black theaters and was even shown to mixed-race audiences in normally whites-only theaters in New Orleans. The proceeds, however, were still short of what was needed for another film, and raising money proved even more difficult than before.

The Johnsons were partly victims of their own success, which spawned rival companies that diluted the already limited pool of money available for investment in race movies. Chief among these were the white-owned Reol Productions Company of New York and Ebony Pictures, run by black filmmaker Luther Pollard. Pollard boasted that his films were "without those situations that are usually attributed to the American Negro,"[15] but his comedies showed the same timeworn stereotypes. At least one was shut down in Chicago because local black leaders termed it degrading.

Reol and Ebony, however, at least produced motion pictures. Some thirty fly-by-night black companies raised funds with promises of lavish productions that were never made. George Johnson kept a meticulous record of such companies, including their slick brochures on which he had written "no records of any film produced."[16]

Other factors worked against the Lincoln company. A postwar economic recession meant even less spending money for blacks. A nationwide influenza epidemic reduced audiences. Universal Studios told Noble Johnson that if he was to work for them, he could no longer make pictures for Lincoln.

Last Lincoln Films

There would be, however, two more films—*A Man's Duty* and *By Right of Birth*. The latter was unusual in that it explored the sensitive subject of blacks "passing" for white. The film was a critical success but a financial failure, and in 1923 the company ceased operations. Thomas Cripps writes that Lincoln had "provided a black aesthetic statement where otherwise there would have been a void."[17] That statement was that the American dream of prosperity and upward mobility was open to blacks and that their own determination and hard work could overcome barriers, even those posed by the white majority.

Of the Johnsons' many rivals, the most serious, and the one who finally supplanted them as the nation's leading black filmmaker, was Oscar Micheaux. One of eleven children of parents who were former slaves, Micheaux was reared in Kansas and at the age of twenty-one established a farm in an otherwise all-white area of South Dakota. He recorded his experience in a 1913 novel, *The Conquest*, copies of which he sold to neighboring white farmers and in nearby towns.

In 1915, having lost his farm during a severe drought, Micheaux moved to Sioux City, Iowa, where he established the Western Book and Supply Company. He rewrote his novel, retitled it *The Homesteader*, and sold it door-to-door throughout the Midwest. In early 1918 the Johnson brothers read the book and thought it would make an ideal film.

Contract negotiations between the author and the filmmakers broke down because Micheaux insisted on directing the film himself. Micheaux then set out to make the film on his own: He moved to Chicago, took over a studio once used by William Selig,

Micheaux on Micheaux

About three years before his death in 1951, pioneer black filmmaker Oscar Micheaux wrote to S.W. Garlington, a reporter for the *New York Amsterdam News*, in answer to a question of why he had made movies from his own books instead of from other stories. Garlington printed Micheaux's reply in the filmmaker's obituary:

> "I'm tired of reading about the Negro in an inferior position in society. I want to see them in dignified roles. . . . Also, I want to see the white man and the white woman as the villains. . . . I want to see the Negro pictured in books just like he lives. . . .

> "But," he added, "if you write that way, the white book publishers won't publish your scripts . . . so I formed my own book publishing firm and write my own books, and Negroes like them, too, because three of them are best sellers."

Source: Quoted in S.W. Garlington, "Oscar Micheaux, Producer, Dies," *New York Amsterdam News*, April 7, 1951. http://shorock.com/arts/micheaux/clipping/nyamstnews.html.

and reorganized his company as the Micheaux Film and Book Company. He turned for funding to the midwestern farmers and merchants who had bought his book and raised enough money for the project.

"A Rough Negro"

With speed and bravado that both impressed and intimidated George Johnson, who called him "a rough Negro who has got his hands on some cash,"[18] Micheaux filmed *The Homesteader* and scheduled its Chicago debut on February 20, 1919.

Micheaux was a relentless promoter. His prerelease advertisement in the *Chicago Defender* boasted that the film was "destined to mark a new epoch in the achievements of the Darker Races."[19] And one of the promotional brochures he used to raise money promised that "nothing would make more people anxious to see a picture than a litho [poster] reading: 'SHALL RACES INTERMARRY.'"[20]

An important African American film director of the 1920s, Oscar Micheaux (pictured) sought to portray blacks in a dignified light.

Whether it was because of the quality of the film or the extent of promotion, *The Homesteader* was a financial success. Micheaux was able to do what the Johnson brothers had not—clear enough to finance his next project, *Within Our Gates*. He based this film on the case of Leo Frank, a Jew lynched by a Georgia mob in 1915, and rewrote it as the story of the lynching of a black farmer, unjustly accused of murder, and his wife.

Troubled Premiere

Within Our Gates premiered in January 1920 at Chicago's Vendome Theater, but not without a struggle. Chicago had experienced a race riot only a few months before, and many city leaders, both black and white, believed the film's inflammatory subject could spark more violence and tried to block its release. The mayor and police chief thought otherwise, and the screening was allowed.

Despite the controversy and Micheaux's steady drumbeat of promotion, *Within Our Gates* was not a success. The lynching theme scared off theater owners and distributors, and the film received almost no screenings in the South.

Undaunted, Micheaux followed up with a success, *The Brute,* starring black boxer Sam Langford, and scored another with *Body and Soul* in 1924. The latter is noteworthy for two reasons: It marked the screen debut of black star Paul Robeson, and it is arguably Micheaux's most powerful film, a harsh, realistic depiction of the victimization of ghetto blacks by fellow blacks, including unscrupulous ministers.

Most of Micheaux's films were less high-minded and original; many frankly copied standard white themes. Even his star actors were copies, billed as the "black [Rudolph] Valentino" or the "sepia [Jean] Harlow." Furthermore, many of his featured actors were light-skinned, leading his critics to dismiss them as "light-brights."[21]

Tight Budgets

Micheaux's films were technically unsophisticated, even less so than *The Birth of a Nation* ten years earlier. Filming and editing were usually completed in six months or less. Camera operators were hired by the day, and most scenes were shot in one "take," or performed only once. To save money on building sets, Micheaux frequently talked wealthy black friends into letting him use their homes, sometimes repaying them by giving them small roles.

In the second half of the 1920s, Micheaux had new competition. The Dunbar Amusement Company set up shop in an

Oscar Micheaux's Message

The most successful producer of "race movies," films made explicitly for black audiences, was Oscar Micheaux. Micheaux was frequently criticized, however, for concentrating on middle-class black issues while ignoring the reality in which most of black America lived. Donald Bogle offers this evaluation of Micheaux:

> What remains Oscar Micheaux's greatest contribution . . . is often viewed by contemporary black audiences as his severest shortcoming. That his films reflected the interests and outlooks of the black bourgeoisie [middle class] will no doubt always be held against him. His films never concentrated on the ghetto. They did not deal with racial misery and decay. But that didn't mean they did not acknowledge racial problems. Usually, though, the films concentrated on upright middle-class protagonists. At times, one may feel he's created a world that's part fantasy, part reflective of a segment of the black bourgeoisie. He seems determined to depict blacks as just as affluent, just as educated, just as "cultured" as white America.

Source: Donald Bogle, *Toms, Coons, Mulattoes, Mammies & Bucks*. New York: Continuum, 2006, p. 115.

old Vitagraph studio in New York City, and the Colored Players went into production in Philadelphia. The Colored Players' first effort, *A Prince of His Race*, was little more than a standard melodrama, but the next two, *Ten Nights in a Barroom* and *Scar of Shame*, were two of the most genuine portrayals of the black community of the silent era.

A poster for an Oscar Micheaux race film shows the director's preference for using light-skinned black actors.

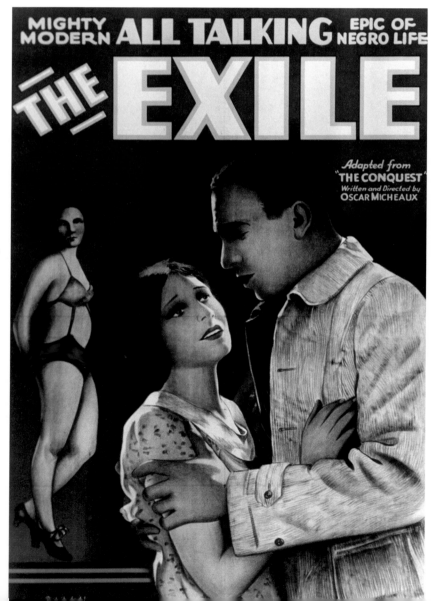

MIGHTY MODERN **ALL TALKING** EPIC OF NEGRO LIFE

THE EXILE

Adapted from **"THE CONQUEST"** *Written and Directed by* **OSCAR MICHEAUX**

Ten Nights in a Barroom was a black retelling of the nineteenth-century stage melodrama that was based on an 1854 anti-alcohol novel. The new version took an uncompromising look at the effects of alcohol addiction, not only on blacks as individuals and on black families, but also on black neighborhoods suffering from the violence and lawlessness of bootleggers.

Scar of Shame

Scar of Shame was even more disturbing to black audiences because it explored the sensitive subject of castes within the black community. Light-skinned concert pianist and music teacher Alvin rescues Louise, a darker-skinned girl who is being beaten by her brutal, drunken stepfather. They fall in love and marry, but ultimately are pulled apart by their differences in the black social order. Rather than having the lovers triumph over their difficulties, the movie ends with Louise committing suicide and Alvin marrying a fair-skinned student.

Scar of Shame in 1929 and Micheaux's *Wages of Sin* the same year and *The Exile* in 1931 were among the last of the silent race movies. Independent black producers could not afford the equipment needed to make the new and popular sound pictures, and few black theater owners could afford the necessary renovations. Only Micheaux would survive the change, making movies as late as 1948. But he and other pioneers such as the Johnson brothers had shown that there was an audience for black films and that black filmmakers could achieve at least some commercial success.

Chapter Three

Singers and Servants

With the coming of sound to motion pictures, white film producers relying on stereotypes assumed that the best roles for blacks would be in musicals. But the big musicals of the early "talkie" days did not meet financial expectations, and black actors soon settled into another typecast role, that of servant.

As the 1930s progressed, however, a black star system developed alongside one for white actors, and the servants gradually became more integral characters in films. At the same time, their attitudes toward their employers changed from meek servility to trusted confidante to something approaching—but never quite reaching—equality.

Parallel to these developments, civil rights groups, white liberals, and a handful of actors grew increasingly outspoken in their protests over the more degrading portrayals of blacks on-screen. Hollywood finally listened, and by the time the United States entered World War II, the heavy reliance on the southern stereotypes that had marked blacks since the beginning of motion pictures had begun to fade.

The Old South Lives On

At the start of the decade, however, Hollywood thought of blacks almost entirely in an Old South context that was clearly reflected in the early all-black musicals. Two major studios competed to produce the first film in this category. Director King Vidor, a white Texan, citing the "sincerity and fervor of [blacks'] religious expression,"[22] talked Metro-Goldwyn-Mayer (MGM) into producing a black musical. At the same time, producer William Fox sought to expand a proposed short film on black life in the post–Civil War South.

Fox made it to the screen first with *Hearts in Dixie* in the spring of 1929. Starring Clarence Muse as a dignified tenant farmer, Bernice Pilot as his daughter, and in his first major role, Stepin Fetchit (born Lincoln Perry) as his shiftless son-in-law, the movie was basically a simple drama interspersed with scenes of dancing and songs performed by a black choir.

The 1929 film *Hearts in Dixie* was the first in the highly popular genre of musicals featuring an all-black cast.

The film was praised by white critics and hailed by some black writers as a major step forward. The actors agreed. "This [a black film also appealing to whites] is the game we must build ourselves into,"[23] said Muse. Others were not so sure. Critic Henry Dobb wrote that the "tragedy is not the tragedy in the film but the tragedy of the film; the tragedy of these untainted folk strutting their stuff to the required pattern, playing their parts as the white man likes to believe."[24]

Hallelujah!

Vidor's *Hallelujah!*, released in August 1929, took a harder look at black life in the South, including the stress placed on families split by migration to the North. Like *Hearts in Dixie, Hallelujah!* was well received by critics, although some black writers complained that it went too far in contrasting the simple, moral lifestyle of the South with the wickedness of the North's urban ghetto.

Faint Praise for *Green Pastures*

Critics were divided in their opinions of *The Green Pastures*, the 1936 film that depicted biblical stories as told by a black minister to a group of children at Sunday school. Some thought the film charming, while others considered it disrespectful of Christianity. Some found its portrayal of blacks to be quaint, but others saw it as condescending. Critic Margaret Ferrand Thorp, writing ten years after the film came out, saw both points of view:

> The producer [Jack Warner] is ready to protect the Negro and avoid stirring race hatreds by keeping off the modern screen such villainous Negroes as appeared in Griffith's *The Birth of a Nation*, but the best he thinks he can do beyond that is to make the Negro so amusing and agreeable that an audience is always pleased at the appearance of a black face. A Negro may also appear in a position where he excites no laughter, but sympathy. . . . The all-Negro *The Green Pastures*, for all its originality and, at some points, elevation, permitted, however, a certain feeling of superiority on the part of the [white] audience.

Source: Quoted in Peter Noble, *The Negro in Films.* New York: Arno, 1970, p. 9.

Radio-Keith-Orpheum (RKO) jumped on what it thought was a bandwagon later the same year with *St. Louis Blues* starring the great blues singer Bessie Smith. But none of these three early musicals fared as well at the box office as they did with critics. Black films would be rare throughout the 1930s, and many of the nation's most talented singers and dancers were relegated to "shorts" that would take a backseat to other Hollywood products.

Not until 1936 would another major black film, *The Green Pastures*, be produced. Based on a popular stage play, it retells the biblical Old Testament as interpreted by children in a black Sunday school. Heaven becomes an eternal fish-fry where "De Lawd" hands out cigars. White critics were lukewarm, and most black critics were hostile. Some writers condemned the film as blasphemous. Like the major black films that had preceded it, *The Green Pastures* was a commercial disappointment, but it made a star of Rex Ingram, whose multiple roles included De Lawd, and it was the movie debut of Eddie Anderson, later to gain fame as comedian Jack Benny's sidekick valet, Rochester.

More Servant Roles

It is noteworthy that Anderson was best known for playing a servant. That indeed was the role most of the black stars of the 1930s were stuck with. As Donald Bogle writes, "No other period in motion-picture history could boast of more black faces carrying mops and pails or lifting pots and pans than the Depression years."[25] Some black intellectuals criticized actors for accepting such demeaning parts, but the actors defended themselves, saying that their roles emphasized admirable traits. Louise Beavers, for example, famous for roles as meek, sympathetic maids, said she wanted "my public to know me as playing these loving character parts."[26]

There was not much to admire, however, in the traits portrayed by Fetchit, who took his name from his old vaudeville act titled "Step and Fetch It." He made fifty-four films from 1925 to 1976, in most of which he played the same character—a slow-moving, dim-witted, head-scratching buffoon, exasperating to his masters, to whom he usually responded, "Yassuh, Boss," when admonished.

Fetchit's bowing-and-scraping character was scorned by black critics but loved by audiences, particularly when he was teamed

Stepin Fetchit, shown here in an undated movie still, was known for playing the black buffoon in films of the 1930s.

with white comedian Will Rogers. Whites laughed at his antics, but blacks were perceptive enough to see that he was, in his own way, overplaying his roles and slyly poking fun at his own stereotype.

Fetchit's Successors

Fetchit's success, however, led Hollywood to cast others in the same undignified mold. Willie Best, early in his film career, even adopted a Fetchit-like name, "Sleep 'n Eat," a play on the slur that all a black man needed to keep him happy was a place to sleep and enough to eat. Mantan Moreland, a moon-faced actor with prominent, protruding eyes, was frequently cast as a sidekick to a brainier character such as detective Charlie Chan and would tremble with fear and run at the first sign of danger.

Two of Fetchit's successors were unique in that their acting was secondary to other talents—music in the case of Louis Armstrong and dance in that of Bill "Bojangles" Robinson. While black musicians were often included in Hollywood movies as nightclub acts apart from the main plot, jazz trumpeter Armstrong was famous enough that he frequently had speaking roles. His acting, however, seemed to consist of what film historian Peter Noble calls "movie mugging . . . always to assume the startled and slightly inane expression . . . conventionally regarded as 'typically Negroid.'"[27]

Robinson, a spectacular dancer, reached the height of his movie fame in four films opposite child star Shirley Temple. The most popular were *The Little Colonel* (1935) and *The Littlest Rebel* (1936), in which the producers returned to the Civil War theme, portraying Robinson as the faithful family retainer who becomes a guardian and protector of Temple.

The pairing of Robinson and Temple served to illustrate how cautious Hollywood was in depicting interaction between black males and white females. No one objected to Robinson, the good servant, dancing with little Shirley. However, when Armstrong was partnered with white singer Martha Raye (in blackface) in a musical number, it drew widespread protest.

Rochester and Benny

It was Eddie "Rochester" Anderson who took the black male sidekick role in a new direction. Wisecracking and back-talking in his trademark gravelly voice, Rochester frequently outwits Jack Benny and never hesitates to point out his boss's shortcomings, notably his legendary penny-pinching. He may have been a servant to Benny, but he was hardly servile.

By the time Anderson perfected his back-talking character in the late 1930s, black female servants in the movies had been doing the same for years. The decade had not started out that way, however. Popular white actresses such as Mae West and Jean Harlow generally played glamorous characters attended by black maids with names like Beulah, Petunia, or Jemima. Mistresses sometimes confided in their maids, but there was never a hint of equality.

Louise Beavers excelled in such roles, which led to her most important film—and a landmark in black film history—1934's

Imitation of Life. Beavers plays a widow, Delilah, who is taken in as a housekeeper by a white widow, Bea. Soon the pair are running a home-based pancake flour business and raising their daughters; the business and the girls grow and thrive over several years. Delilah remains meek and subservient; when the now-wealthy Bea tells her partner that she can afford her own house, Delilah protests that she just wants to remain a cook. All she wishes for is a simple life ending with an extravagant funeral.

Much of the drama of the plot revolves around Delilah's relationship with her light-skinned daughter, Peola, who is ashamed of being black and tries to pass for white, a sensitive issue addressed for the first time in a major Hollywood film. When she is accidentally exposed by her mother, Peola rages against the system only to be told by the submissive Delilah, "Open up and say, 'Lord, I bows my head.'"[28] The character of Delilah was faulted by many critics, and the movie is often cited as an example of segregation-era films that show blacks eagerly adopting the values of white culture, but Beavers's performance drew rave reviews, and many thought she should have been nominated for an Academy Award.

McDaniel's Success

The change came only a year later when Hattie McDaniel played Katherine Hepburn's maid in *Alice Adams*. McDaniel's trademark persona—a strong, outspoken, no-nonsense black woman—had emerged when she played Stepin Fetchit's wife in *Judge Priest* in 1934. In *Alice Adams* her outspokenness is directed not at her black husband but at her white mistress. Her strong opinions are clear even when she expresses herself only with a disdainful grunt or a baleful glare. She is very much her own person and does not care who knows it.

In *The Mad Miss Manton* (1938) McDaniel keeps her society girl mistress Barbara Stanwyck in her place with acid comments. Once, when McDaniel answers the phone, Stanwyck giggles "It must be my date." "Sounds more like a pipsqueak to me," McDaniel shoots back. Describing the scene, Bogle writes, "Just talking back was a triumph of sorts, and Hattie McDaniel was doing what every black maid in America must have wanted to do at one time or another."[29]

The "Sunny Side" of Slavery

The idea of the pre–Civil War South as an idyllic time and place where slaves worked contentedly for masters who treated them kindly and looked after their simple needs endured throughout the early decades of the motion picture industry. Nowhere was it more evident than in *Hearts in Dixie*, one of the first all-black musicals produced after the advent of talking pictures.

Film historian Donald Bogle points out the folly of this glorification of slavery:

> Here were characters living in shacks and working from sunrise to sunset, and always, instead of suffering or misery, they seemed to be floating on some euphoric high brought on, one would assume, by cotton fields and spirituals. "The spirit of the Southern Negro . . . is cleverly captured," wrote [a] *New York Times* film critic. "It is something restful, a talking and singing picture that is in a gentler mood and truthful in its reflection of black men of those days down yonder in the cornfields." . . . Once again the perpetually happy-go-lucky Negro was presented to movie audiences—stamped with a seal of Establishment approval!

Source: Donald Bogle, *Toms, Coons, Mulattoes, Mammies & Bucks*. New York: Continuum, 2006, p. 27.

McDaniel was just warming up, however, for the signature role of blacks in the 1930s, widely considered the ultimate servant portrayal—Mammy in *Gone with the Wind* (1939). Black characters were integral to the plot of Margaret Mitchell's wildly popular Civil War–era novel, and producer David Selznick was determined that they "come out decidedly on the right hand [positive] side of the ledger"[30] in the film version.

McDaniel is so closely identified with Mammy that it is hard to imagine anyone else playing the role. There was intense casting competition, however; Eleanor Roosevelt, wife of President Franklin D. Roosevelt, even wrote Selznick that the part should go to her personal maid. McDaniel got the part largely at the insistence of her friend Clark Gable, who was to play the lead white male role of Rhett Butler.

Mammy and Scarlett

When Selznick saw what McDaniel brought to the film, however, he knew he had made the right choice and even altered the script to give her special brand of humor more time onscreen. Mammy is a maid to Scarlett O'Hara, the spoiled rich white heroine, but she is also a mother figure, advising, scolding, or comforting Scarlett as the occasion demands. She is fiercely protective, shoving shiftless loafers aside as she and Scarlett walk along a street in

Hattie McDaniel (shown with Vivien Leigh) was the first black to win an Academy Award for her portrayal of Mammy in *Gone with the Wind*.

A Charge of Slander

—————————■—————————

Much like *The Birth of a Nation* a generation earlier, *Gone with the Wind* in 1939 was a spectacular success and is included in many lists of the best films ever made. But like its predecessor, *Gone with the Wind* came under fire for its portrayal of blacks. One of the strongest statements came from the New York State Committee of the American Communist Party:

> *Gone with the Wind* revives every foul slander against the Negro people, every stock-in-trade lie of the Southern lynchers. Well-dressed in a slick package of sentimentality for the old "noble" traditions of the South, this movie is a rabid indictment against the Negro people. The historical struggle for democracy which we have come to cherish so dearly is vilified and condemned. . . . Not only is this vicious picture calculated to provoke race riots, but also to cause sectional strife between the North and the South just when the growth of the labour and progressive movement has made possible unity of Negro and white, on behalf of the common interests of both.

Source: Quoted in Peter Noble, *The Negro in Films*. New York: Arno, 1970, p. 79.

postwar Atlanta. She is quick to see inside the soul of every person she meets and heaps scorn on those who do not meet her standards.

McDaniel's Mammy was the strongest, most sympathetic black character in any film up to that time. She brought to the role not only the no-nonsense humor that had made her famous, but also a dramatic intensity that drew praise from critics and won the hearts of audiences. Black leaders, however, had a problem. They joined in the praise for McDaniel but could hardly overlook the other blacks in the film. In contrast to the dignified Mammy, there was the hysterical, good-for-nothing pickaninny Prissy; the servile Pork; and the clownish Uncle Peter. Typical was the *Pittsburgh Courier*'s review, which praised the film's artistry and McDaniel's performance but complained that "much of it was distasteful to the Negro race."[31] Black criticism was muted when her performance earned McDaniel the first Academy Award ever given to a black actor, the Oscar for Best Supporting Actress, in 1940.

The Emperor Jones

While servants made up the bulk of major black roles in the 1930s, there were significant exceptions. In *The Emperor Jones* (1933), Paul Robeson plays a former railroad porter who escapes from jail to a Caribbean island, where he eventually becomes a king who issues orders to his white former partner. "Black audiences must have felt immensely proud," Bogle writes, to see Robeson "telling them white folks to get outta his way."[32]

Three 1930s films dealt with the explosive subject of lynching. Two, however—*Fury* (1936) and *They Won't Forget* (1937)

Paul Robeson plays the role of Emperor Jones, shown lounging on his throne. *The Emperor Jones* was a movie with a twist: a black man shown as superior to a white man.

—tiptoed around the central issue of race and concentrated on mob violence. *Black Legion* (1937) was more to the point and a surprisingly bold indictment of the Ku Klux Klan by Hollywood standards.

A handful of movies dealt with blacks not as servants, but as criminals. *Bullets or Ballots* (1936) saw Louise Beavers break away from her mammy roles to play the head of an inner-city gambling ring. And Edward Thompson is a hip, wisecracking gunman in *The Petrified Forest* (1936), a forerunner of the street-smart black film heroes of the 1970s. At the other end of the social scale, Clarence Brooks played a dignified, dedicated doctor in *Arrowsmith* (1931), probably the first time a mainstream movie showed a black as an educated professional.

A Decade of Progress

Though films like *Arrowsmith* were in the minority, black roles made significant progress in the 1930s. Blacks were still playing servants at the end of the decade, but Hattie McDaniel's Mammy was a far cry from Louise Beavers's Delilah. And Paul Robeson brought strong dignity to the role of Joe in *Show Boat* (1936) compared with the low comedy of Stepin Fetchit in the same role in the 1929 version.

The United States was approaching a time of dramatic change with the coming of the 1940s. World War II was on the horizon, and with it would come a need for citizens to face a common enemy. Civil rights organizations pressed harder for equality and made it clear that such equality extended to motion pictures. In 1942 Walter White, executive secretary of the NAACP, issued a statement calling on Hollywood to ensure that "the picturization of the Negro [is] not as comic or menial figures but as normal human beings."[33] It would not be an easy task.

Chapter Four

War and Aftermath

It took prodding by the federal government, the NAACP, and its own growing social conscience, but when Hollywood went to war in the 1940s, it took black characters and black actors with it. The results were not all that black leaders had hoped for. Stereotypes kept reappearing, as Cripps writes, like stains in an old carpet, but the wartime movies paved the way for the film industry to address racial issues at the end of the decade in ways that would have been unthinkable ten years earlier.

One of the first signs of change came in 1939, only a few months after the success of *Gone with the Wind*. Actor Clarence Muse and black author Langston Hughes collaborated to write the script for *Way Down South*. It, too, was a sentimental treatment of some aspects of the master-slave relationship, but there were scenes showing black resistance and the cruelties of the slave system.

An even stronger statement came in *In This Our Life* (1941) when Ernest Anderson played a studious black youth unjustly accused of a hit-and-run. His character maintains his poise and integrity until the real culprit confesses. The *New York Times* praised the film for its "brief but frank allusion to racial discrimination."[34]

New Awareness

The United States had not yet entered World War II when *In This Our Life* came out, but international politics had raised Americans' awareness of racial discrimination. The treatment of Jews in Germany and in occupied European countries under Adolf Hitler and the Nazis had demonstrated the extremes to which racism could be taken. The persecution of European Jews made many Americans uncomfortably aware of the historical suffering of blacks in their own country.

When the United States did enter the war in December 1941, a national sense of urgency and the need for unity intensified. The war would call for unprecedented military and manufacturing commitments. Black participation was needed more than ever before.

Black leaders saw this as a clear opportunity to achieve what the *Pittsburgh Courier* called the Double V—victory over enemies

Enforcing Stereotypes

The power of motion pictures to shape attitudes and the extent to which this power was used to the detriment of blacks was discussed in a 1944 article by Lawrence Reddick, a historian at Fisk University in Nashville, Tennessee:

> The treatment of the Negro by the [film industry] is inaccurate and unfair. Directly and indirectly it establishes associations and drives deeper into the public mind the stereotype conception of the Negro. By building up this unfavourable conception, the movies operate to thwart the advancement of the Negro, to humiliate him, to weaken his drive for equality and to spread indifference, contempt and hatred for him and his cause. This great agency for the communication of ideas and information, therefore, functions as a powerful instrument for maintaining the racial subordination of the Negro people.

Source: Quoted in Peter Noble, *The Negro in Films*. New York: Arno, 1970, p. 7.

overseas and victory over racism at home. Walter White, executive secretary of the NAACP, declared that blacks would "fight for liberties here while waging war against dictators abroad."[35] His task, writes Cripps, was to find a way for "short-run national necessity to be shaped into a long-run politics of civil rights."[36]

The NAACP View

Ever since *The Birth of a Nation*, the NAACP had been trying to get Hollywood to give blacks more meaningful roles and to show them, White said, "as a normal human being and integral part of human life and activity."[37] To White that meant depicting blacks

The NAACP's Movie Message

The National Association for the Advancement of Colored People (NAACP) had long been concerned with the image of blacks depicted in most Hollywood films as well as in the all-black "race movies." Of particular concern was the issue of black actors who agreed to play stereotypical or demeaning roles. In 1942 NAACP executive secretary Walter White issued what he called a "statement to the Negro public, particularly Los Angeles":

> Our utmost wisdom and intelligence must be used by Negro actors, present and future, and by the Negro public generally on the pledges which have been made by the motion picture industry to broaden the treatment of the Negro in films. . . . Negroes must realize that there are three vitally important phases of the subject. First and most important is picturization of the Negro not as comic and menial figures but as normal human beings. Growing out of this is the second phase of more acting roles for Negroes in motion pictures. Third is the matter of employment of qualified colored men and women in the technical end of the production. As for those actors in Hollywood who can play only comic or servant roles, I trust they will not let their own interests spoil the opportunity we now have to correct a lot of things from which Negroes have suffered in the past in the movies.

Source: Quoted in Thomas Cripps, *Slow Fade to Black*. New York: Oxford University Press, 1993, p. 387.

as members of an integrated society, taking their places alongside whites in schools, churches, the workplace, and other routine activities of everyday life.

White had the federal government as an ally. Washington knew that the country would need large numbers of blacks as well as whites in the armed forces and on factory assembly lines. Officials were worried that black Americans might be susceptible to enemy propaganda telling them this was a white man's war in which they had no stake.

Roosevelt realized that the government needed an organized effort to convey the message of unity and equality. In June 1942 he created the Office of War Information (OWI), charged among many other duties with producing newsreels and overseeing the content of motion pictures. The OWI pressed Hollywood not only to include more black roles but also to see that such roles did not perpetuate derogatory stereotypes. While the OWI disavowed any intent to solve the country's racial problems, it was nevertheless, according to a staff manual, "particularly interested in all appearances of dark-skinned races."[38]

Hollywood Allies

White also had allies in Hollywood. Producers Daryl Zanuck at Twentieth Century Fox and independent Walter Wanger were genuinely sympathetic to White's cause. So were some big-name stars such as Humphrey Bogart and John Garfield and prominent directors such as Mervyn LeRoy and Frank Capra.

But the movement had opponents, as well. Conservatives in Congress, mainly southern Democrats, accused some of White's Hollywood sympathizers of having Communist Party leanings. Some major producers, such as Frank Freeman at Paramount Pictures, resented what they felt to be interference.

Ironically, much of the opposition came from established black actors such as Willie Best, Hattie McDaniel, and Eddie Anderson. Their livelihoods depended on the kind of roles that White sought to eliminate from film. Anderson would later dismiss White as "an Eastern phoney trying to be white."[39]

The servant roles indeed almost disappeared. Wartime pictures tended to shy away from portraying rich whites with black maids and butlers. Some traditional roles, however, made it onto

Part of the War Effort

◼

The entry of the United States into World War II created a massive increase in manufacturing and, along with it, a massive need for labor. Many jobs from which blacks had traditionally been barred were now open to them. The government wanted all Americans to feel that they were part of the war effort, and one of the methods considered important was to portray ethnic minorities in a more favorable light than in the past.

The governmental entity that oversaw the depiction of minorities in motion pictures and other forms of entertainment was the Office of War Information. The work of the OWI and the importance attached to it was recounted in a 1943 *New York Times* article:

> Two major studios, Metro-Goldwyn-Mayer and Twentieth Century Fox, in producing pictures with all-Negro casts, are following the desires of Washington in making such films at this time. Decisions to produce the pictures, it is stated, followed official expression that the Administration [of President Franklin D. Roosevelt] felt that its program for increased employment of Negro citizens in certain heretofore restricted fields of industry would be helped by a general distribution of important pictures in which Negroes played a major part.

Source: Quoted in Donald Bogle, *Toms, Coons, Mulattoes, Mammies & Bucks*. New York: Continuum, 2006, p. 137.

the screen. Best played his usual bumbling part in *The Kansan* in 1943, and McDaniel was once more a maid in *Since You Went Away* the following year.

The Musicals

The black musicals made an occasional appearance. Paul Robeson, who had not made a film in the United States since 1936, was enticed home to star in the black segment of *Tales of Manhattan* in 1942. But the scenes of happy blacks singing and dancing in the cotton fields drew widespread ridicule, and Robeson said, "I wouldn't blame any Negro for picketing this film."[40]

Cabin in the Sky received a similar reception the following year. This film placed blacks in a fantasy world much as in *The Green*

Pastures. It starred Anderson as a gambler whose soul is the subject of a duel between heaven and hell. Despite praise for the performances of Anderson, Ethel Waters, Lena Horne, Rex Ingram, and others, *Time* magazine dismissed their characters as "picturesque, Sambo-like entertainers."[41]

The other all-black musical of 1943 was the very different *Stormy Weather.* Featuring the aging Bill "Bojangles" Robinson and Lena Horne, the film portrayed the history of black entertainers over the previous twenty-five years. Even though it avoided the stereotypes of *Cabin in the Sky*, it risked, Thomas Cripps writes, "portraying African America as a happy place with happy problems."[42] Its modern theme and jazzy music, however, had wide appeal for audiences.

Lena Horne (seated) starred with Eddie Anderson (standing, center) in the 1943 black musical movie *Cabin in the Sky*.

The "Rugged Loner"

The goal of White and the OWI, however, was not to make black films, but to see blacks in meaningful roles alongside whites. But if those roles were not to be the traditional ones of servants or entertainers, what were they to be? In Cripps's view, Hollywood borrowed a stock character from the western film genre—the "rugged loner versus society." In westerns, that might be the mysterious gunman who comes to the aid of peaceful townspeople; the new black protagonist would interact with a small company of whites and, in the process, enrich their lives. This theme, writes Cripps, "would define a black place in American life for the next generation."[43]

World War II provided the ideal dramatic setting for such a theme. The most outstanding examples were *Sahara, Crash Dive,* and *Bataan* in 1943 and *Lifeboat* the following year. All featured black characters whose bravery and integrity were important contributions to the story line.

Sahara was different from the others in that the black character was not an American but a Sudanese sergeant, played by Rex Ingram, who falls in with an American tank crew and other Allied soldiers separated from the main force in the North African desert. It is the black character the rest look to for guidance across the desert, and ultimately he is killed trying to save his new friends.

Black Heroes

In both *Crash Dive* and *Lifeboat*, black actors play Americans but are not yet pictured as equal in status with whites. *Crash Dive* features a character based on the real-life Dorie Miller, a kitchen assistant on the USS *Arizona* who manned a machine gun during the attack on Pearl Harbor and shot down at least one Japanese plane. In *Lifeboat*, a small group of survivors adrift on the ocean includes a steward first called Charcoal and then more respectfully Joe when the rest learn that he had saved one of the women and her child from drowning. When some of the others team up to kill a German sailor, Joe refuses, having once witnessed a lynching.

Bataan puts its black character on a more even footing with whites than the others. Wesley, played by Kenneth Spencer, is a former minister who has been trained in the army as a demolitions expert and is part of a lost patrol in the Philippines. He offers an eloquent prayer over the grave of a fallen comrade and at last is killed with the rest. The *New York Times* wrote, "Kenneth Spencer has quiet strength and simple dignity as a Negro soldier from the engineers—a character whose placement in the picture is one of the outstanding merits of it."[44]

Such characters, however, portrayed blacks in a white world but not as an integral part of that world. Blacks and whites could be thrown together by wartime necessity in a boat or on patrol, but not live, work, or attend school together in the same neighborhood. "No one," writes Cripps, "could imagine any other arrangement, at least for now."[45]

New Themes

When the war ended in 1945, it thus became more difficult to find "rugged loner" roles for black actors. The dominant theme of films was no longer national unity, but adjustment to peacetime, especially the problems of returning veterans. Most of white America was concerned with the experience of whites, not blacks, however. In fact, one film dealing with the subject, *Till the End of Time* (1946), changed all the characters from the original book from black to white.

White and the NAACP began to lose their influence in Hollywood. The OWI's motion picture office had been closed in 1944, partly due to pressure from conservative congressmen. White proposed the establishment of a permanent NAACP film agency, but the idea got a cool reception from even his closest allies in Hollywood.

Indeed, the end of the war seemed to bring a dramatic decrease in "serious" black roles and a return to conservative, traditional portrayals. Producers were more concerned with profits and tended to avoid anything controversial, especially as the Un-American Activities Committee of the U.S. House of Representatives began investigating alleged Communists in the film industry. As Harry Cohn at Columbia Pictures put it, "Give me somethin' I can use and nothing controversial—like niggers or God."[46]

So it was that projects such as *The Dark Garden*, about Jewish and black doctors, were never filmed. Even the movie version of the jazzy Broadway show *St. Louis Woman* was canceled because it was deemed too hot to handle. In *Duel in the Sun* in 1946, Butterfly McQueen played a maid much the same way she had played the pickaninny Prissy in *Gone with the Wind*.

Song of the South

The best example of what was considered a safe black role was that of kindly old Uncle Remus in Walt Disney's *Song of the South*. Based on the Joel Chandler Harris stories, the film featured Uncle Remus telling white children tales of Br'er Rabbit, Br'er Fox, and Br'er Bear, all animated figures.

Song of the South embodied everything the NAACP had been fighting against. The organization said that it gave "an impression

The 1946 Disney movie *Song of the South* (a scene from which is shown here) was highly criticized by black leaders for its happy-go-lucky portrayal of slaves.

of an idyllic master-slave relationship which is a distortion of the fact."[47] The *New York Times* lambasted the producer for "putting out such a story in this troubled day and age" and added, "Put down that mint julep, Mr. Disney!"[48]

White audiences, however, loved the film and especially James Baskett, the veteran vaudeville actor assigned to the role by Disney after Rex Ingram turned it down. Even some black critics such as the NAACP's Gloster Current, while deploring the movie, called Baskett "artistic and dynamic."[49] As it had been with Hattie McDaniel, criticism of Baskett was muted when he received an honorary Academy Award for the performance.

But while the flame of race consciousness flickered, it never went out. The modest success of wartime documentaries such as *The Negro Soldier* and *Teamwork* led to similar postwar efforts to highlight racial issues. Although such films as *To Secure These Rights*, *The Color of Man*, and *The Quiet One* were seldom seen in theaters, they found outlets in union halls, schools, and public libraries.

The Message Movies

Such documentaries, although the public was largely unaware of them, were praised by film critics and by organizations such as the NAACP and the League of Women Voters. Perhaps this led Hollywood to risk controversial subject matter once again, and an eruption of "message" pictures followed—*Home of the Brave, Lost Boundaries, Pinky, Intruder in the Dust* (all 1949), and *No Way Out* (1950). These films, writes Cripps, "signaled the opening of an era warmed by a sense of urgency [and] also a sense that the four years of maturing since the war placed them on the verge of the most important peacetime era of race relations since Reconstruction."[50]

The way had been paved by the success of two films dealing with anti-Semitism—*Gentleman's Agreement* and *Crossfire*—and by the 1947 film *Body and Soul*, in which a black ex-boxer played a pivotal role. *Home of the Brave*, the first of the message pictures, is the story of a shell-shocked veteran remarkable in that the central character was deliberately rescripted by the studio from a Jewish man to a black man. It contains some of the strongest language heard up to that point from a black character, as the veteran tells a white psychiatrist, "I learned that if you're colored, you stink. You're not like other people. You're—you're alone. You're something strange, different. . . . Well, you make us different, you rats."[51]

Lost Boundaries revisited the theme of blacks passing for white. When a couple's true ethnicity is revealed to their New England neighbors, the burden is felt most keenly by their children. *Pinky* echoed the same theme in a film that earned Ethel Waters an Academy Award nomination. Both films, however, cast white actors such as Mel Ferrer and Jeanne Crain in black roles, reflecting both the studios' caution and their reliance on stars who would attract white audiences.

New Look at Lynching

Intruder in the Dust took up the subject of lynching in a way different from any previous film. The character of Lucas Beauchamp, played by Juano Hernandez, is not the meek, stoic, unjustly accused black victim of the past. Instead, he is proud to the point of arrogance, dressed in suit and tie, a gold toothpick in his mouth, striding confidently into a Mississippi general store under the malignant gaze of whites. While he is ultimately cleared of murder, he never begs or pleads, but rather treats his captors with a quiet scorn. At the end of the film, realizing an innocent man was almost lynched, an attorney says, "He wasn't in trouble. *We* were in trouble."[52]

The new decade opened with *No Way Out*, the vehicle that launched Sidney Poitier to stardom as a young doctor who must treat a pair of wounded racist criminals. Even when shot by one of them, he saves the man's life, but he's no all-forgiving saint. "Don't you think I'd like to put the rest of these bullets through his head?" he says. "I can't . . . because I've got to live, too."[53] *No Way Out* was also noteworthy in that it also provided a breakout role for Ruby Dee, who would costar with Poitier in some of the decade's most important films.

In the space of eleven years, Hollywood had gone from Hattie McDaniel's Mammy to Sidney Poitier's Dr. Brooks. The country had undergone an equally dramatic change. World War II had produced, if imperfectly, a sense of unity and an awareness of the inequality that undermined such unity. Motion pictures had done much to lay bare the problem of racial discrimination, and they would do even more in the decade to come.

Chapter Five

The Troubled Times

The 1950s and 1960s were turbulent decades for American blacks. Events piled swiftly upon one another, moving from nonviolent boycotts, sit-ins, freedom rides, and voter registration drives to increasing militancy, waves of urban riots, and shouts for "Black Power." The motion picture industry did little to push this upheaval. Rather, it was pulled along by the tide.

Hollywood had done its small part with its message movies of the late 1940s, but the spark came from within the black community. Those who had fought overseas and worked in factories to free others now wanted to free themselves. They were more vocal about what they wanted and economically more able to get it.

However, as the civil rights movement began to heat up in the early 1950s, Hollywood went in the opposite direction, retreating to the bland style of the films that had followed World War II. It was not entirely the film industry's fault. Mainstream America had become more affluent and content and mostly did not want that contentment disturbed by "message" films. Also, the House Un-American Activities Committee investigations of Hollywood had resulted in several prominent directors being "blacklisted," or denied work, and others were fearful of exclusion if their films were deemed too controversial.

Token Blacks

There were plenty of films with black characters in the 1950s but few black themes. Hollywood thought it sufficient, Cripps writes, to "[limit] racial discourse to the admission of a single iconic [symbolic] black into a white circle."[54] In later years this practice, in the film or any other industry, would be known as tokenism.

Nevertheless, during the 1950s several black actors reached a level of unprecedented stardom. Their films, for the most part, were "safe," and although black critics might have complained, the new middle-class black audiences embraced them, as did whites.

Blacks had played strong characters before, but none had ever been so central to a major Hollywood film as Ethel Waters in *Member of the Wedding* (1952). As the housekeeper Bernice, she comforts, advises, and protects two white children. She is a mammy figure, but unlike Hattie McDaniel's characters, she is strong without being strident and gentle without being sugary. She is nevertheless a traditional mammy and thus more of an echo of the past than a sign of the future.

Carmen Jones

The first big all-black production of the decade was *Carmen Jones*, the 1954 film version of the Broadway musical that translated George Bizet's opera *Carmen* as a black musical. Although it featured established stars including singers Pearl Bailey and Harry Belafonte, the film was dominated by Dorothy Dandridge in the title role. She so excelled as the seductive and ultimately self-destructive Carmen that she earned an Academy Award nomination for Best Actress, the first for a black woman in that category.

The film itself, however, had nothing to do with black issues. The plot primarily involves a love triangle that could be projected onto almost any ethnic group. Racial attitudes did dictate, however, that there would be very little physical intimacy in this version of the love story. Black sexuality, especially black male sexuality, was taboo in Hollywood.

This policy is especially evident in *Island in the Sun* (1957). The Alec Waugh novel had probed racial tensions on a Caribbean is-

Harry Belafonte and Dorothy Dandridge (pictured) starred in a large all-black movie musical, *Carmen Jones,* based on the opera *Carmen* by Georges Bizet.

land and included love affairs between a black man and white woman and between a black woman and white man. Filming took place, however, during a landmark civil rights event in the United States, the Montgomery, Alabama, bus boycott led by the Reverend Martin Luther King Jr. Producer Darryl Zanuck opted to tone down the film's interracial story line. One prominent character, a militant lawyer, was eliminated altogether, and the love scenes between Dandridge and white actor John Justin and between Belafonte and white actress Joan Fontaine were tame indeed. Of the scene in which Justin confesses his love for Dandridge, the actress later said, "We had to fight to say the word *love.*"[55]

Belafonte and Sidney Poitier, the major black male stars of the 1950s, both suffered from Hollywood's timidity. This was especially true in Belafonte's case because he relied on his exotic good looks and singing voice more than acting ability. In only one film, *Odds Against Tomorrow* (1959), which Belafonte personally produced, did he emerge as a multidimensional character, a musician down on his luck who falls in with a gang of bank robbers. When the robbery fails, their fragile partnership is torn apart by racism. The message, rare in the 1950s, was that racism left unchecked could also tear the country apart.

Poitier's Popularity

It was Poitier who emerged as the most popular black actor of the decade. After *No Way Out*, he played some supporting roles before scoring big again in *The Blackboard Jungle* (1954). One of the more honest and hard-hitting films of the 1950s, this is a hard look, not at racism, but at unrest and violence among urban youth. But even though Poitier's student character joins others in baiting a white teacher, he chooses in the end to defend the teacher when the man is attacked by a classmate.

The role was a departure for Poitier. Up to then he had played calm, restrained, even-tempered characters, but in this film he lashes out against an unjust system and defiantly refuses to succumb to it. In the end, however, his innate goodness determines his actions, and goodness and intelligence would mark most of his roles for the rest of his career.

Poitier, writes Bogle, "was fast becoming a national symbol of brotherly love."[56] This assessment was borne out in *Edge of the City* with Ruby Dee in 1957 and *The Defiant Ones* the next year. The central plot line of both was the same—the forging of a bond between black and white men.

In the earlier film Poitier is a railroad worker who befriends and gets a job for a white drifter. Later, when he defends his new friend in a fight, he is killed, stabbed in the back by his friend's foe. In *The Defiant Ones* the men are bound, not by friendship, but literally—they are prison escapees chained together. A comradeship does develop, however, and Poitier eventually sacrifices his freedom to save his friend.

Slow to Change

Poitier was nominated for an Academy Award for *The Defiant Ones*, but many blacks saw his willingness to play a man who sacrifices himself for a white man as a sellout. The 1950s were waning, and the promises of equality through integration had not been fulfilled. The national race-relations debate was increasingly tense, but Hollywood would be slow to reflect this. As the 1960s began, safe films were the norm. *Flaming Star* in 1960 made one of the strongest statements about racism, but it dealt with American Indians rather than blacks. Also in this period, Hollywood released some feature films about the trials of light-skinned black women, but these characters were often played by white actresses, just as in the 1940s. And accompanying the increasing integration of professional sports, some celebrated black athletes such as baseball player Jackie Robinson, tennis star Althea Gibson, boxer

Sidney Poitier (left) rescues Tony Curtis in *The Defiant Ones*. The film was remarkable for showing a bond between black and white men.

Jersey Joe Walcott, and football player Woody Strode tried their hand at acting. But none of their films carried a strong message, and Gibson, far from bucking stereotypes, played a maid. It was as if, black actor Brock Peters said, Hollywood "was scared . . . to try a really black picture."[57]

There were some good, well-intentioned attempts at realism, the first of which was *A Raisin in the Sun* (1961), which film historian Thomas Cripps calls the only major film that "dared to portray a genuine core of black culture."[58] Poitier, in a another departure from his cool, calm image, plays a frustrated limousine driver who cries out to his long-suffering wife played by Ruby Dee, "That ain't no kind of a job . . . that ain't nothing at all."[59]

Sidney Poitier (right) and Ruby Dee (center) head an outstanding cast in the 1961 film *A Raisin in the Sun*, the first movie to realistically portray black life.

Praise for *Raisin*

◾

When Lorraine Hansberry's play *A Raisin in the Sun* opened on Broadway early in 1959, producer David Susskind immediately began working to secure the movie rights. He wrote to a Columbia Pictures executive that "I have an inside track on this property as a consequence of my relationship with the author and her attorney" and that the play was "a profoundly moving story of negro life in which, for once, the race issue is not paramount."

After the film came out, Susskind received not only good reviews but several letters of praise. One, from a television executive, said, "Perhaps more in this industry than any other we are judged by what we do when we have the opportunity to do it. . . . You and your associates have produced an even more immediate and compelling piece than the play itself. It is indeed a credit to the movie industry and certainly will be to this country overseas."

Source: Quoted in Mark Reid, *Redefining Black Film*. Berkeley and Los Angeles: University of California Press, 1993, pp. 57, 60.

A Raisin in the Sun sought to capture the hopelessness and bottled-up frustration of poor urban blacks who yearn to escape the ghetto but cannot see a way out. In a way that no film before it had accomplished, it examined the strain such despair placed on black families.

Independent Films

Other films of the early 1960s that were more in tune with the times came not from the major studios but from independent filmmakers. In *Shadows* (1961), for example, a light-skinned black woman and a white man fall in love. In a twist from the usual plots in such films, she does not disclose her ethnicity not because she is ashamed of being black but because she assumes that it does not matter. Sadly, she finds out otherwise when her boyfriend deserts her after learning the truth.

Two years later, *The Cool World* looked at the subculture of youth gangs in New York City's Harlem district, portrayed as a culture of sex, drugs, and violence largely ignored by the affluent whites who live just a few blocks away. Another previously ignored subject—interracial marriage—was taken up in *One Potato, Two Potato*. In this film, society's inability to accept such a marriage is shown when custody of the white wife's daughter by a previous marriage is awarded to her white biological father, despite the fact that he had deserted her and her mother. Finally, in 1964 *Nothing but a Man* spoke out against not only white discrimination in the South but also the fear and timidity of blacks that allowed it.

The general attitude of Hollywood toward blacks is best reflected in a series of highly successful Poitier films, starting with *Lilies of the Field* (1963), which earned him the first-ever Best Actor Academy Award for a black actor. His character breaks no new ground, however; he is again the lone black in an all-white group, this time a traveling construction worker who encounters a band of nuns who believe he has been divinely sent to help them build

Poitier on His Oscar

In 1964 Sidney Poitier became the first African American to win the Academy Award for Best Actor for his role in *Lilies of the Field*. While some saw his victory as a turning point in American race relations, Poitier disagreed:

> Did I say to myself, "This country is waking up and beginning to recognize that certain changes are inevitable"? No, I did not. I knew that we hadn't "overcome," because I was still the only one. My career was unique in all of Hollywood. I knew that I was a one-man show, and it simply shouldn't be that way. And yet in a way I found the accolade itself quite natural. I wasn't surprised that such good things were happening to me, because I'd never seen myself as less than I am. When I realized that I could be a better than utilitarian actor, I realized that I had the responsibility, not as a black man, but as an artist, to exercise tremendous discipline. I knew the public would take my measure, and that was constantly in my calculations.

Source: Sidney Poitier, *The Measure of a Man*. San Francisco: HarperCollins, 2001, p. 107.

a chapel. His character is the perfect black hero for white audiences—warm-hearted, earnest, dependable, nonthreatening, and on the road out when the job is done.

Still a Servant

Black critics pointed out that Poitier's role in *Lilies of the Field* was close to that of a servant. The same held true for his next two major films, *The Slender Thread* and *A Patch of Blue*, both released in 1965. In the former he is a crisis-clinic volunteer who answers a phone call from a woman who has taken pills to commit suicide. He keeps her on the phone until she can be rescued. Although race plays no part in the plot, Poitier's role is that of a helper. In *A Patch of Blue* he befriends a blind white teenage girl, once more in a helping capacity, but their relationship remains sterile and chaste.

In 1967 Poitier starred in *To Sir, with Love* as a teacher in an integrated English high school, a far cry from his juvenile-delinquent role in *The Blackboard Jungle*. While race is mentioned, it is not a focus of the film, and Poitier, according to a *New York Times* review "gives a quaint example of being proper and turning the other cheek."[60]

Perhaps the film that epitomized Poitier's style and Hollywood's approach to race in the 1960s is *Guess Who's Coming to Dinner*. This immensely popular movie begins with the engagement of a black man and white woman (both conveniently well educated, affluent, and sophisticated) and focuses on their parents' reactions to the young couple's announcement. Despite the serious themes raised by the script, the film is played mostly as a comedy of manners. Indeed, one character sums things up by saying, "Civil rights is one thing but this here is something else," and the *New York Times* said the film "seems to be about something much more serious and challenging than it actually is."[61]

Criticism for Poitier

When *Guess Who's Coming to Dinner* was released in 1967, racial violence was erupting in major cities across the country, and the question in many minds was whether blacks and whites could coexist. The movie was out of step with the times, and so was Poitier. In a 1967 article, *New York Times* writer Clifford Mason asked,

"Why does white America love Sidney Poitier so?" Mason's answer was that he specialized in sympathetic, unthreatening roles, which were "essentially the same role, the antiseptic, one-dimensional hero."[62] Mason's criticism extended even to one of Poitier's most militant roles of the decade, a black detective helping to solve a murder in the Deep South in *In the Heat of the Night*.

If Poitier exemplified the past, the future was represented by Jim Brown, a professional football legend who retired at the peak of his game and went into movies. He was big, black, and, in Bogle's word, played "baaaddd" roles, and the "fact that he lacked enough talent to play them didn't matter much."[63]

Brown swaggered through such films as *The Dirty Dozen* (1967), *Ice Station Zebra* (1968), and *Riot* (1969). Many of his roles were of the "lone black" variety, but with a difference. Brown was always the man of action in the group, quick to use raw, physical power as well

Guess Who's Coming to Dinner provided a look at interracial dating in 1967. The film featured Sidney Poitier, Spencer Tracy, and Katharine Hepburn.

Poitier's Rebuttal

In 1967, shortly after Sidney Poitier played an upper-middle-class black intellectual in *Guess Who's Coming to Dinner*, Clifford Mason wrote a story for the *New York Times* headlined "Why Does White America Love Sidney Poitier So?" Mason's point was that Poitier was not helping the cause of black Americans by playing such tame roles. In his autobiography, Poitier replied:

> All I can say is that there's a place for people who are angry and defiant, and sometimes they serve a purpose, but that's never been my role. And I have to say, too, that I have great respect for the kinds of people who are able to recycle their anger and put it to different uses. On the other hand, even Martin Luther King, Jr., and Mahatma Gandhi, who certainly didn't appear angry when they burst upon the world, would have never burst upon the world in the first place if they hadn't, at one time in their lives, gone through much, much anger and much, much resentment, and much, much anguish. . . . Well, I certainly don't live [King's and Gandhi's ideals] every day, but I believe in it with my whole being. If I were asked for an evaluation of myself, I would readily admit to my sins . . . and the reason I can do that and not be ashamed is that I'm willing almost always to try my best.

Source: Sidney Poitier, *The Measure of a Man*. San Francisco: HarperCollins, 2001, p. 124.

as cunning. Black audiences responded to Brown's heroes the way whites did to Sean Connery's James Bond character.

New Militancy

Brown was not alone in reflecting the militancy of the late 1960s. A series of films, starting with *Up Tight* in 1967, captured the increasing rejection of integration and embrace of separatism in black America. But while *Up Tight* showed black guerrilla fighters in the streets of Cleveland, *The Learning Tree* (1969) took a slightly less confrontational tone. In this film Gordon Parks, the first black director of a major American film, told the story of his boyhood

A young James Earl Jones plays a boxer in *The Great White Hope,* a movie that tackled the sensitive issue of integrated sexual relationships.

in Kansas. The story is anything but idyllic, as the creek where he swims turns red with the blood of a murdered black man.

The increasing willingness of Hollywood to take on sensitive racial themes is further exemplified by *The Great White Hope* (1970). This fictionalized story of black boxer Jack Johnson and his sexual relationship with white women won James Earl Jones a Best Actor nomination, the first black actor so honored since Poitier.

The last years of the decade were filled with all kinds of social upheaval and protest, much of it angry. "In 1960, Negroes were quietly asking for their rights," writes Bogle. "By 1969, blacks were demanding them."[64] The civil rights movement's spokesman for nonviolence, Martin Luther King Jr., was assassinated in 1968, and firebrands such as Stokely Carmichael and H. Rap Brown grabbed the spotlight to preach a different message—violent rejection of white-dominated society. It was time for a new type of black film, and this time Hollywood was ready.

Chapter Six

Blaxploitation and Beyond

The anger of many black Americans, so seldom reflected in the motion pictures of the 1960s, exploded onto the screen in 1971, unleashing a flood of films in which black heroes and a few black heroines not only battled established authority, but won. As with all floods, however, the so-called blaxploitation wave receded and Hollywood got back to business as usual, setting the stage for the next revolution.

The man who opened the floodgate was actor and director Melvin Van Peebles. Dissatisfied with *Watermelon Man*, a fantasy he directed about the experience of a white man who wakes up one day as a black man, he set out "to do a movie that told it like it is. How I saw things."[65] With a relatively modest budget of $500,000—$50,000 borrowed from popular comedian and television actor Bill Cosby—he made *Sweet Sweetback's Baadasssss Song*, which, writes Rutgers University professor Jesse Rhines, "changed the course of African American film production and the depiction of African Americans on screen."[66]

The film follows the flight of the title character after he brutally murders two white policeman whom he sees beating a defenseless black youth. Rejecting a predictable ending in which Sweetback is killed or captured, Van Peebles (who also plays the

Melvin Van Peebles looks through the camera lens on the set of *Watermelon Man*, his 1971 fantasy film created for black audiences.

lead role) lets his hero escape after a series of scenes filled with sex and violence. He is not in the least sorry for what he has done, and the on-screen message at the conclusion reads, "A baadasssss nigger is coming back to collect some dues."[67]

The film opened in 1971 in only two theaters but soon caught on with black audiences, especially young males. The word spread, and Van Peebles's film eventually generated a profit of more than $10 million. The movie appalled most critics, black and white alike. But black critic Lerone Bennett, who deplored the content, conceded that such a shocking film was "an obligatory step for anyone who wants to go further and make the first revolutionary black film."[68]

Shaft and *Super Fly*

Other films quickly capitalized on *Sweetback*'s success. Gordon Parks moved from the slow pace of *The Learning Tree* to the up-tempo *Shaft* in 1971, starring Richard Roundtree as the detective clad in black leather who does things his own way. Shaft was a new kind of black hero who not only refused to be intimidated by whites but also rejected the model of assimilation into white society embodied in Sidney Poitier's roles.

Shaft was an even bigger box office success than *Sweetback*, thanks in part to its Academy Award–winning musical score by Isaac Hayes. The movie did well with both black and white audiences but was particularly popular with inner-city blacks. Donald Bogle writes that John Shaft looked "like a [black] brother they had all seen many times before but *never* on the screen."[69]

The third groundbreaking film in the blaxploitation genre was *Super Fly* (1972), directed by Parks's son, Gordon Parks Jr. It went a step further than *Sweetback* and *Shaft* in that the hero, Youngblood

The Making of *Sweetback*

Melvin Van Peebles's *Sweet Sweetback's Baadasssss Song* was a surprise hit in 1971 and a huge financial success for Van Peebles, who had retained ownership of the negative of the film. In an interview many years later, he said his success was more due to poverty than to any business sense:

> People talk about *Sweetback*. Man, I was just hoping I would get the money back so that the people I had borrowed from, buddies of mine, wouldn't kill me. No biggie. People say, "You're such a financial wizard. With *Sweetback* you own the film negative." I said, "I ain't got partners. Not because I was brilliant, but because nobody would do it with me." I played the role of Sweetback not for any reason except that I could find no one who would play it for me who knew anything about cinema. An actor would say, "Put in a few more lines for *Sweetback*." I'd say, "Well, he doesn't talk a lot." . . . [Advising black filmmakers to retain control of their product] ain't what I do. I knock the door down and let the people get in any way they can get in. I would not intimate that everybody else follow my way of doing things. There are other ways of doing things—you get it to work, how you want it to be, and that's fine.

Source: Quoted in George Alexander, *Why We Make Movies*. New York: Harlem Moon, 2003, pp. 21, 24.

Priest, is neither an avenger nor a detective, but an ordinary street criminal, a cocaine dealer in New York City. He is not a rebel and does not have a political agenda. He just wants to make as much money as he can and get out alive, which he manages to do.

The themes at work in *Super Fly* directly contradict those of the integration films—cooperation, compassion, and patience. Instead, *Super Fly* seems to glorify the idea that the end justifies the means, even if those means are illegal and involve getting ahead at others' expense.

Another common aspect of *Sweetback, Shaft*, and *Super Fly* is that women are more possessions than people, sexual objects to be used and discarded. Some films, however, featured women in

Gordon Parks's Advice

Gordon Parks already had established his credentials as an award-winning photographer for *Life* magazine when he turned to filmmaking in 1964. His autobiographical 1969 film *The Learning Tree* won critical praise, but his biggest hit was *Shaft* (1971), one of the groundbreaking "blaxploitation" films. Once, asked for his advice for young directors, he said:

To do anything well, you have to have a purpose other than just money. You have to have good feelings about the universe, about people, about helping it become a better universe. Become what God wanted us to become when he put us in this universe—to make a contribution. You should not just take up space here without showing your thanks to the power for having put us here, and that's what I try to do. I try to make my day worthwhile, my life worthwhile. If you don't have good thoughts about good things, you'll never make good photographs. You're not going to make good pictures and you're not going to write good books or anything else. You're not going to write good music. You might think that you're being successful, but in the end you're not unless you're making some sincere contribution—especially to our youth, because our youth are tomorrow. Without our youth, there is no tomorrow.

Source: Quoted in George Alexander, *Why We Make Movies*. New York: Harlem Moon, 2003, p. 14.

"bad nigger"[70] roles, as they were called by University of California professor Charles Henry. Actors Pam Grier and Tamara Dobson are both deadly and sexy in such films as *Foxy* and *Cleopatra Jones*, but unlike most of their male counterparts, they have respectable goals, such as clearing up the drug trade in their neighborhoods.

The Imitators

The success of the early blaxploitation films led to a steady stream of imitators. Between 1971 and 1974, it is estimated that one-fourth of all movies made in the United States followed similar formulas. That does not mean they originated in the black community, however: More than 80 percent were written, directed, and produced by whites.

Many black leaders were outraged by the constant parade of thugs, prostitutes, drug dealers, and addicts across the nation's screens and accused white filmmakers of sensationalism and exploitation. Their protests had little effect, but blaxploitation eventually was its own worst enemy. The plots kept repeating themselves, audiences grew bored, profits shrank, and filmmakers turned to other projects. Blaxploitation films, however, had made their marks, leaving—for better or worse—a specific image of urban black culture in the public mind.

It was not, however, the only image. Although there were few good roles for black women, three actresses made the most of what there was. Diana Ross, former lead singer in the Motown supergroup the Supremes, scored a Best Actress Academy Award nomination for *Lady Sings the Blues* (1972), a fictionalized biography of jazz singer Billie Holiday. Two years later, Diahann Carroll received a similar nomination for *Claudine*, the simply told story of the trials of a welfare mother in New York City.

Sounder

One of Ross's rivals for the 1972 award was another black actress, Cicely Tyson, for *Sounder*. That film, set in the South in the 1930s, movingly dramatizes the strong bonds of love and respect among members of a black farm family, one of the first such depictions of black family life. It was indeed one of the most outstanding motion pictures of the 1970s, earning Oscar nominations not only for Tyson, but for Best Picture, black screenplay writer Lonnie Elder III, and Best Actor for Paul Winfield, who played the family father.

The primary focus of black films after the waning of blaxploitation, however, was comedy. The groundwork had been laid in 1972 with the success of *Buck and the Preacher*, which marked the debut of Poitier as a director. He also costarred in the film with Harry Belafonte as two freed slaves who outwit whites who attempt to return them to slavery. It was an example of what Bogle calls the "crossover" film, one characteristic of which is to "strip the black film of any raw political content."[71]

Buck and the Preacher did not get good reviews, and Poitier was wise enough in subsequent 1970s comedies such as *Uptown Saturday Night, Let's Do It Again*, and *Stir Crazy* to leave most of the comedy to more experienced actors. He acted in the first two, but those films were carried by black comics Bill Cosby, Flip Wilson, and the emerging black star of the decade, Richard Pryor, respectively.

Richard Pryor

Pryor was hardly a newcomer. He had been performing as a nightclub comedian since 1963 and had perfected an image of someone who would say and do anything, no matter how outrageous or profane. It was the kind of character that he could not, as yet, play on-screen, but he still came across as wild and utterly unpredictable. He was just as disdainful of authority as Sweetback, but instead of fitting Henry's description of the "bad nigger," Pryor was what Donald Bogle calls the "crazy nigger."[72]

His first part in a major film was the serious dramatic role as the edgy drug addict Piano Man in *Lady Sings the Blues*, which won him critical respect. Cowriting and acting credits in comic films followed, including *Car Wash*, before Pryor teamed up with Gene Wilder in *Silver Streak* (1976). His depiction of Grover Muldoon, a quick-witted, jive-talking thief, made Pryor a major star throughout the 1980s and 1990s.

Not even Pryor's talents, however, could save *The Wiz*, the 1978 film version of the all-black Broadway hit. At a cost of $24 million, it was the most expensive musical made to date. With an all-star cast that included not only Pryor but also Diana Ross, Lena Horne, Nipsey Russell, and nineteen-year-old Michael Jackson as the Scarecrow, it seemed failproof.

The outrageous comedian Richard Pryor (left) teamed with Gene Wilder for *Silver Streak* in 1976. The two paired up for several popular "buddy" films.

But fail it did. Critics lambasted *The Wiz*, many complaining that Ross at thirty-four was just too old for the role of Dorothy. Film historian Charles Harpole called it "one of the decade's biggest failures."[73] It was a commercial disaster as well, taking in only $13.6 million in ticket sales.

The combination of bad reviews and financial losses may have convinced Hollywood that there was no longer a mass audience for all-black movies. Such films, which had been a staple of the 1970s, all but vanished in the next decade. Roles for black actors declined overall and were mostly limited to supporting parts. Academy Award nominations mirrored the trend. Between 1980 and 1990 only three black actors were nominated for leading roles, nine for supporting roles.

"Buddy" Movies

Many of the supporting roles came in what are called "buddy" movies—the often unlikely pairing of two people, often from being awed by the people he encounters, he uses his race as a weapon, throwing it in their faces and watching them back off. His character, Axel Foley, proved so popular that three sequels of *Beverly Hills Cop* were made, the latest due in 2009.

Although Murphy and many other black males achieved success in the 1980s, it was not a good time for black women in film. Few films offered black actresses roles in which they could make an impact. The major exception was *The Color Purple* (1985), which emerged as the most forthright and controversial black film of the decade.

The Color Purple

Based on Alice Walker's Pulitzer Prize–winning novel, *The Color Purple* explores the often abusive relationships between black women and black men. Whoopi Goldberg, playing the long-suffering Celie, was the only black actress nominated for an Acad-

Whoopi Goldberg (pictured) was nominated for an Academy Award for her role as Celie in the black-themed drama *The Color Purple* in 1985.

emy Award in a leading role in the 1980s, but her costars Margaret Avery and Oprah Winfrey were also nominated for supporting roles.

Controversy arose over the film's depiction of black men, which some critics labeled one-sided. Their depiction as brutes, it was charged, was just as wrong in 1985 as it was seventy years earlier in *The Birth of a Nation*. Critics and audiences were split over *The Color Purple*, and the split was evident when the film failed to win any Oscars despite eleven nominations.

Although *The Color Purple* was one of the only black-themed motion pictures of the 1980s, several others were based on race relations. But while blacks enjoyed prominent roles, many of these stories concentrated more on the white experience. For instance, *Cry Freedom*, a 1987 feature about South African activist Steve Biko, earned up-and-coming Denzel Washington an Oscar nomination for Best Supporting Actor, but much of the movie was given over to his white journalist friend. Likewise, when Washington won the Best Supporting Actor Academy Award for *Glory* in 1989, most of the plot had to do with the black Civil War company's white officer.

Another such film, *A Dry White Season*, addressed racism in South Africa, but the most sympathetic character is a white schoolteacher. The film was notable, however, in that it was the first major Hollywood movie directed by a black woman, Euzhan Palcy.

Then, in 1987, only five years after earning a master's degree in film and television studies at New York University, a black director made his presence known with the surprise hit *She's Gotta Have It*. His name was Shelton Jackson Lee, better known as "Spike," and he would take black film in a new, bold direction in the coming decades.

Chapter Seven

Spike and His Friends

The 1990s were the most exciting, innovative, and prosperous years for African Americans in film in the almost one hundred years since black actors first appeared on-screen. More blacks were finding success, both in front of and behind the cameras, than ever before. The films they were making were not only Hollywood blockbusters but thoughtful, funny, and sometimes irreverent views of black culture.

The bold tone of the decade was largely due to the influence of a single man, director Spike Lee, whose films revolutionized the way black America was portrayed on the screen. Three years after his graduation from NYU, he began work on *She's Gotta Have It*, the story of an independent black woman choosing between three very different lovers. That film created a stir, as did its successor, *School Daze*, an ironic look at class consciousness within an all-black university. But the reaction was nothing like the sensation caused by *Do the Right Thing* in 1989.

The film takes place on a single day during a heat wave on a single street in a Brooklyn neighborhood of New York City. Lee fills the screen with people who are instantly recognizable to urban black audiences: old people sitting on front stoops, angry young men, young women flaunting their sexuality, working-class whites with racist tendencies. Tensions build, and a young black man is accidentally killed by white policemen. At this point pizza deliveryman Mookie (played by Lee), who struggles with both middle-class and militant values, loses control and touches off a riot in which his boss's pizza parlor is burned to the ground.

Praise and Concern

Chicago Sun-Times critic Roger Ebert wrote that the film "comes closer to reflecting the current state of race relations in America than any other movie of our time."[74] Other reviewers deplored the portrayal of violence, and some civic leaders worried that it would spark riots. At the heart of the controversy was disagreement about whether Lee was condemning the violence or excusing it as justified. By ending the film with opposing quotations on

The Injection of Violence

Spike Lee's first two major films, *She's Gotta Have It* and *School Daze*, did not prepare viewers for the violent conclusion to *Do the Right Thing*, when a black youth is killed by police and a race riot ensues. Indeed, in his journal, Lee wrote that he would "introduce the subject [of racism] lightly. People will expect another humorous film from Spike Lee."

He decided to make the film take a darker turn in late December after hearing a news report about an assault on two black youths in a white neighborhood in New York City. He wrote, "While I was in the grocery today, I heard a radio newscast that two Black youths had been beaten up by a gang of white youths in Bensonhurst. The two Black kids were hospitalized. They were collecting bottles and cans when they got jumped. This happened on Christmas night. Just the other day some Black kids fired up a white cab driver in Harlem. New York City is tense with racial hatred. Can you imagine if these incidents had taken place in the summer, on the hottest day of the year? I'd be a fool not to work the subject of racism into *Do the Right Thing*."

Source: Quoted in Mark A. Reid, *Redefining Black Film*. Berkeley and Los Angeles: University of California Press, 1993, p. 104.

violence from Martin Luther King and Malcolm X, he seemed to be leaving the choice up to the viewer.

Lee went on to make dozens of feature films on every aspect of black culture, from sports (*He Got Game*, 1998) to music (*Mo' Better Blues*, 1990) to political activism (*Get on the Bus*, 1996). All were controversial, but none more than *Malcolm X* (1992), based on the autobiography of the inflammatory Black Muslim leader assassinated in 1965. Some people said the movie glorified the black nationalist; others said it did not glorify him enough. As usual, Lee seemed to be an observer, presenting the story and letting viewers draw their own conclusions.

Director Spike Lee (far right) gave himself an acting part in his controversial film *Do the Right Thing*. The 1989 movie featured racial tensions and violence.

Spotlight on Racism

In the months following the release of Spike Lee's *Do the Right Thing*, some critics complained that the portrayal of white racists and the violence at the film's conclusion upset many white viewers. To this, Lee replied,

> How do you think Black people have felt for 80 years watching stuff like *Birth of a Nation* . . . and we go on and on. Black people have had to live under this thing for 400 years. If white people have to squirm for two hours watching this film, that's great. I think it's a good kind of squirming, because for the most part the movies today are just mindless entertainment; they don't make you think. We made this film so we could put the spotlight on racism and say everything is NOT okay, that this is not the land of milk and honey and truth and justice. We should stop hiding from the issue of racism.

Source: Quoted in Jesse Rhines, *Black Film/White Money*. New Brunswick, NJ: Rutgers University Press, 1996, p. 112.

Publicly, however, he was always quick to speak out against Hollywood's hesitancy to make serious black films and, when it did, black audiences' refusal to support them. "We're still relegated to these ghettos," he said. "You don't see movies about Sojourner Truth or Matthew Henson [abolitionist and explorer, respectively, in the 1800s] or Black science fiction or a Black thriller. The studios say, 'We're not buying that.' They say, 'Do you have something with drugs or a rapper, something we can put [rap singer] Nelly in?'"[75] Such comments have alienated Hollywood insiders and may be a factor in Lee's record of only two Oscar nominations (Best Screenplay for *Do the Right Thing* and Best Documentary for *4 Little Girls* in 1979) and no Oscars.

Following Lee's Lead

Several black directors followed Lee's lead. Immediately after he saw *Do the Right Thing*, John Singleton went to work on the screenplay for *Boyz 'n the Hood*, a 1991 story about gang violence

Denzel Washington played the title role in Spike Lee's 1992 biography *Malcolm X*. The film was as inflammatory as its subject.

in South Central Los Angeles. The film earned Singleton Academy Award nominations for Best Director—the youngest person and only black ever so honored—and for Best Screenplay.

The same year saw the release of *New Jack City*, produced and directed by Melvin Van Peebles' son, Mario. There are similarities between Mario's film and his father's *Sweetback*. Both are uncompromising views of inner-city life. The key difference is that, while Sweetback flouts the law and succeeds, *New Jack City*'s drug lord Nino is gunned down at the film's end. This theme—urban crime and violence is a dead end—would recur in many movies of the 1990s.

A similar fate awaits black gang leader Slim in *A Rage in Harlem*, directed by Bill Duke. And Caine, the young drug dealer in *Menace II Society* (1993), directed by Albert and Allen Hughes, tries to escape the ghetto and make a new life but is killed in a drive-by shooting. Such films portray the daily reality of violence as both the new breed of black directors and those who lived in the inner city saw it. Harvard University professor Henry Louis Gates comments on the violence depicted on the screen, saying, "You don't know whether you're watching a nightmare or the nightly news."[76]

Other Views

Not all the new black films concentrated on modern ghetto life. Carl Franklin's *Devil in a Blue Dress* re-created the South Central Los Angeles of the 1940s in an unusual crime-thriller that was reminiscent of the private detective films of that era, only from a black point of view. George Tillman's *Soul Food* (1997) is a gentle story about the love and tensions among members of a middle-class family in Chicago. The film proved that there were compelling black stories to be told beyond the inner city. Melvin Donaldson, a California professor and film historian, calls it "one of the most memorable films to present contemporary black family life."[77]

Giving Back

Bill Duke followed a successful career as an actor (*Car Wash, American Gigolo, Menace II Society, Predator, Bird on a Wire*) with an equally successful career as a director. In addition to *A Rage in Harlem* and *Deep Cover*, he has directed television episodes of *Hill Street Blues, Miami Vice*, and *Fame*.

In 1998, after becoming chair of the Department of Radio, Television, and Film at Howard University in Washington, D.C., Duke began a program of mentoring young blacks aspiring to careers in motion pictures. Classes of thirty-five would-be actors or directors attended a ten-week course "to study acting and industry survival techniques."

In talking about black films, Duke extends the meaning of the term. "There are a lot of films I want to make about America, films that have to do with issues that *affect* black people, but don't involve them," he said. "They happen in corporate offices and in halls of justice, in congressional halls—the politics of this country. Black people have no access to this reality. Those are things I want to talk about, the films I want to make. . . . I want to be able to make a film . . . because I'm the best director for the film."

Source: Quoted in Melvin Donaldson, *Black Directors in Hollywood*. Austin: University of Texas Press, 2003, p. 287.

Indeed the militancy of black films seemed to have significantly mellowed. Perhaps the best example was *The Best Man* in 1999. Directed by Spike Lee's younger cousin Malcolm, the film dealt not with drug lords in the ghetto but with educated, middle-class black professionals, including a novelist, a social worker, and a television producer. It is a movie about blacks, but is not a black movie. The characters have human problems, but not exclusively black problems. The film is so different from those of Spike Lee, who coproduced it, that *Village Voice* critic Amy Taubin writes that Spike "has never directed a film that goes down as easily as this one does."[78]

New Stars

The wave of black films in the 1990s provided new opportunities and led to stardom for a host of black actors, mostly male actors. Denzel Washington was already famous for his work in *Cry Freedom* and *Glory*, but the decade would bring him two more Academy Award nominations—for *Malcolm X* and *The Hurricane*—and lead roles in such hits as *Mo' Better Blues, The Pelican Brief, Crimson Tide*, and *He Got Game*. Ruggedly handsome, he was a favorite of black women but, like other black actors before him, he was given few romantic roles in a Hollywood still reluctant to show black male sexuality.

Morgan Freeman solidified his status as one of America's most popular actors, gaining an Academy Award Best Actor nomination as the world-weary convict of *The Shawshank Redemption* in 1994. Also earning a Best Actor nomination was Laurence Fishburne for his role as singer Ike Turner in *What's Love Got to Do with It?* (1993). He was in great demand, appearing in twenty films in the 1990s in roles as diverse as Furious Styles in *Boyz 'n the Hood* and Morpheus in *The Matrix*.

Less-established actors who made names for themselves in the 1990s included Samuel L. Jackson, Cuba Gooding Jr., Wesley Snipes, and Will Smith. Jackson had been a staple of Spike Lee's films, but his career took off when he played Jules Winnfield, the scripture-quoting hit man in *Pulp Fiction* (1994). The performance earned him a Best Supporting Actor Oscar nomination, and he went on to star in such films as *Die Hard with a Vengeance* and *A Time to Kill*. Gooding won the Oscar for Best Supporting

Actor in his role as a pro football player trying to cash in on his talent in *Jerry Maguire* (1996).

Like Jackson, Snipes appeared in several early Spike Lee films, but he began to draw critical acclaim when he played Nino the drug kingpin in *New Jack City*, a role especially written for him. He played many diverse parts, including a basketball hustler in *White Men Can't Jump*, a paraplegic in *The Waterdance*, and a detective sidekick to Sean Connery in *Rising Sun*. But he achieved his greatest success as an action hero, as a policeman in *Boiling Point* and as a vampire hunter in *Blade*, or an action villain, as crime boss Simon Phoenix in *Demolition Man*.

Smith was best known for his lead role in television's *Fresh Prince of Bel-Air* before making a name for himself in back-to-back hits as the cocky fighter pilot in *Independence Day* (1996) and the alien-hunting government agent in *Men in Black* (1997). He proved he could hold his own in a serious lead role in *Enemy of the State* (1998) and ended the decade as one of Hollywood's biggest stars.

The Actresses

The 1990s were not as kind to black actresses, but they still fared much better than during the previous twenty years. The years after *The Color Purple* had not been particularly rewarding for Whoopi Goldberg, but that ended with the romantic fantasy-thriller *Ghost* in 1990. She plays Oda, a fake spiritualist who is terrified when she is actually contacted from beyond the grave by the spirit of Sam, played by Patrick Swayze. She overcomes her fear, becomes a link between Sam and his girlfriend, and helps foil a crime in time to allow the film its bittersweet resolution. Janet Maslin wrote in the *New York Times* that "Ms. Goldberg has found a film role that really suits her, and she makes the most of it."[79] Others agreed, and Goldberg became the second black woman to win an Oscar for Best Supporting Actress.

Other films focused more closely on the lives of black women. In *Daughters of the Dust* (1990), black director Julie Dash relates the conflicts among the women of a South Carolina family in 1902, some members of which are preparing to move north. Much more modern—and commercially successful—was *Waiting to Exhale* (1995), the story of four black women and their relationships with one another and the men in their lives. Directed by veteran black actor Forest Whitaker, the film found a large audience among black women and was yet another triumph for Angela Bassett.

Bassett would prove to be the most popular black actress of the decade. She first came to the public's attention in *Boyz 'n the Hood* and then succeeded in a much more challenging role, that of Malcolm X's wife Betty Shabazz. She then won the role of pop singer Tina Turner in *What's Love Got to Do with It?*, beating out Halle Berry and Robin Givens. Her performance, which one reviewer said "shows off Bassett's ferocity and range,"[80] earned her an Oscar nomination, the first and only time black costars have been nominated for Best Actor and Best Actress. Bassett also received critical and popular acclaim as an older woman in love with a younger man in *How Stella Got Her Groove Back* in 1998.

Black women were thrilled to see a movie that reflected real-life relationships in1995's *Waiting to Exhale*. Here director Forest Whitaker is shown on the movie set.

The Power of Movies

◼

Few black artists in Hollywood have had as much success as Forest Whitaker. As an actor, he earned a Golden Globe nomination for Best Actor as saxophonist Charlie Bird in *Bird* and won the 2007 Academy Award for Best Actor as Idi Amin in *The Last King of Scotland*. He also directed the highly regarded *Waiting to Exhale* in 1995. In an interview, Whitaker gives his views on the power of motion pictures and the care that should be taken by a director:

> Movies can be a myriad of things because movies can transform. . . . By that I mean, in our country we can make people see something and understand something that they never did before. . . . So that's why you have to be careful as to what it is the director does and what it is the director says. . . . I think that I am disappointed in any filmmaker who perpetuates negative stereotypes be they Black, white, Mexican or whatever. Certainly you would think that if it's of your own culture that you would have the sensitivity to know that what you might be doing could be detrimental. . . . So for me, I would hope that Black filmmakers would have the sensitivity to what it is they're projecting and how it can affect people.

Source: Quoted in George Alexander, *Why We Make Movies*. New York: Harlem Moon, 2003, p. 487.

Black women played lead roles in two other feature films of the 1990s, *Eve's Bayou* (1997) and *Beloved* (1998). The first, directed by black actress Kasi Lemmons, tells the story of Eve, a young woman who tries to hold her family together through a series of revelations and crises that end in tragedy. The film was hailed by critics as one of the finest of the decade but received no Academy Award nominations, though critic Roger Ebert wrote, "If it is not nominated for Academy Awards, then the academy is not paying attention."[81]

Oprah's *Beloved*

Beloved, based on the Pulitzer Prize–winning novel by Toni Morrison, received much more attention than *Eve's Bayou*, mainly through the efforts of influential talk-show host and actress Oprah Winfrey, who produced and starred in the film. Winfrey plays Sethe, a former slave with a history of brutalization. In the course of the film it is revealed that when her former master tried to reclaim her, Sethe killed her daughter and tried to kill her other children rather than lose them to slavery. The drama revolves around the appearance ten years later of a young woman who calls herself Beloved and who may or may not be the reincarnation of Sethe's dead daughter.

Critics were divided in their opinions of *Beloved*, and audiences —their expectations perhaps having been raised by the estimated $30 million spent in marketing the film—were mostly disappointed. It was a big loser at the box office and, Bogle writes, "spelled the end of Hollywood's periodic attempt to do more serious films about the black experience in America."[82]

Beloved was not the only film contributing to this development. The $75 million film *Amistad* (1997), about the 1839 mutiny aboard a slave ship, was likewise a financial failure.

The decade did include the rise of several black actors who would reach stardom in the years to come. Halle Berry made her film debut in Spike Lee's *Jungle Fever* (1991) and was featured in *Losing Isaiah* (1995) and *Why Do Fools Fall in Love?* (1998). Jamie Foxx, who started his career in television sketch comedy, made a dramatic impression in the big-screen *Any Given Sunday* (1999). Queen Latifah made the leap from hip-hop to feature films with roles in *Set It Off* (1996) and *The Bone Collector* (1999). And big things were predicted for Jurnee Smollett based on her highly regarded performance in the title role in *Eve's Bayou*.

As the twentieth century ended, Donald Bogle summed up the history of black film by predicting that it had not yet realized its full potential: "Yesterday may not have been great. But the talents of some extraordinary past black film artists make us believe that tomorrow will be better."[83]

Epilogue

Into the New Century

A new century brought fresh faces, both in front of and behind the camera, and equally fresh examinations of the black experience. The established themes and stars were still popular, however, and even a few of the old stereotypes were still to be found.

Rap and hip-hop films were not exactly new, with origins as far back as *Breakin'* and *Beat Street* in 1984, but they multiplied after 2000 as the musical genres began to reach wider audiences. Films such as *8 Mile, Scratch, Beef,* and *Hustle & Flow* were to young black audiences what *Super Fly* had been thirty years earlier. Actor/rappers such as Ice Cube, Tupac Shakur, Terrence Howard, and Jay-Z were the younger generation's icons, as Melvin Van Peebles was in 1971. And the newer films, as did their predecessors, drew severe criticism from those who deplored the music's violence-laden and woman-demeaning lyrics.

The popularity of such films, however, had a spillover effect. Because of their success, says Professor Elayne Rapping of the State University of New York at Buffalo, "black actors like Will Smith, Denzel Washington, and most recently the remarkable Jamie Foxx, have risen in visibility and bankability in more mainstream leading-man roles."[84]

Washington's Oscar

It was, indeed, a great time for black actors, at least male actors. In 2002, for his performance as a crooked policeman in *Training Day* (2001), Washington became the first black honored with the Academy Award for Best Actor since Sidney Poitier thirty-eight years earlier. One of Washington's fellow nominees was Will Smith, who played the title role in Spike Lee's *Ali* (2001), the story of boxing legend Muhammad Ali.

Biographical films, in fact, were the primary vehicles for black male stars. Foxx won the Best Actor Oscar in 2005 for his portrayal of soul singer Ray Charles in *Ray* (2004). One of *his* fellow nominees was Don Cheadle, honored for his performance in *Ho-*

Jamie Foxx (left) and Morgan Freeman proudly show off their Oscars at the 2005 Academy Awards. Foxx won Best Actor for *Ray,* and Freeman received Best Supporting Actor for *Million Dollar Baby*.

tel Rwanda (2004). Forest Whitaker won the Academy Award for Best Actor in 2007 for *The Last King of Scotland* (2006), the story of dictator Idi Amin's rise to power in Uganda. Also nominated in the Best Actor category that year was Will Smith, for his performance in *The Pursuit of Happyness* (2006).

At the 2005 Academy Awards presentation, Foxx not only won for *Ray* but was also an Oscar nominee for Best Supporting Actor for *Collateral*. The winner in that category was Morgan Freeman, for his role as the world-weary boxing trainer in *Million Dollar Baby*.

Academy Award nominations also went to less well-known black actors in the early years of the new century. Djimon Hounsou, a native of the West African country of Benin, was twice nominated for Best Supporting Actor, for *In America* and *Blood Diamond*. Terrence Howard was a Best Actor nominee for his role as a Memphis pimp and would-be hip-hop DJ in *Hustle & Flow*. And Eddie Murphy, better known for his recent light comedies, earned a Best Supporting Actor nomination for his performance as R&B singer "Thunder" Early in *Dreamgirls*.

Altogether, black actors were nominated for Academy Awards in the male acting categories twelve times between 2002 and 2007. Black actresses did not fare as well, but nonetheless garnered four Oscar nominations during the same period, three for Best Supporting Actress. The single nomination for Best Actress in a lead role proved historic: In 2002 Halle Berry became the first black woman to win the Academy Award for Best Actress for her performance as the widow of an executed murderer in *Monster's Ball* (2001).

Few Women's Parts

Otherwise, however, there seemed to be few good parts for black females. "The rise of hip-hop and inner-city movies by and about black men has been almost exclusively a plus for men, not women," Rapping said in 2005. "They are not represented, either as producers or stars, the way men are."[85]

Ironically, it was a rap artist who received one of the three supporting role Oscar nominations that recognized black actresses— Queen Latifah, for *Chicago*. The other nominees were Jennifer Hudson, winner of the Oscar for *Dreamgirls*, and British actress Sophie Okonedo for *Hotel Rwanda*.

Hotel Rwanda, The Last King of Scotland, and *Blood Diamond* were part of a trend in black films of this period, an interest in African history, politics, and culture. Others included *Lumumba*, about the Congolese leader assassinated in 1961; *My Country;* and the South African–themed *Tsotsi* and *Catch a Fire.* "Africa has been under-represented in our literature and our storytelling generally,"[86] says Kevin Macdonald, director of *The Last King of Scotland*, who notes that filmmakers are looking for fresh themes and locations.

But at least one standby genre—action films—remained as popular as ever, even though many of the subjects had been seen before. Samuel L. Jackson starred in a 2000 remake of *Shaft*, Laurence Fishburne made two more *Matrix* films, and Wesley Snipes two more episodes of *Blade. Training Day, Collateral*, and *I Robot* were action-packed, and Denzel Washington played a Harlem drug dealer in 2007's *American Gangster*, which earned veteran Ruby Dee, at age 83, a Best Actress Award nomination. There were more thoughtful films, as well. Cuba Gooding Jr. was featured in two well-received true-to-life movies about blacks in the military: *Men of Honor* is the story of Carl Brashear, the first African American to become a U.S. Navy Master Diver, and *Pearl Harbor* included the story of Doris "Dorie" Miller, who was awarded the Navy Cross for heroism.

The Comedies

The comedians had their day, too. Murphy made *Bowfinger; Norbit;* a remake of the 1960s goofball comedy *The Nutty Professor;* and a sequel to that, *The Klumps.* Other hits included *Head of State, Daddy Daycare*, and Martin Lawrence's *Big Momma's House*, but the comedy most in tune with black culture was Spike Lee's *The Original Kings of Comedy.* This documentary took onstage and backstage looks at a tour in 2000 by comedians Steve Harvey, D.L. Hughley, Cedric the Entertainer, and Bernie Mac. Their irreverent routines about black culture and race relations were reminiscent of Richard Pryor's, and reviewer Esther Iverem praised the "old-school, pre-hip-hop sensibility in the culture."[87]

Other black films in the new century defied easy categorization. *Love and Basketball*, for example, is much more a romantic story than a sports movie. *The Caveman's Valentine*, directed by Kasi Lemmons and starring Samuel L. Jackson, is the offbeat story of a mentally disturbed musician living in a New York City park. And the critically acclaimed *Antwone Fisher*, cited by Spike Lee as the sort of film black audiences should pay more attention to, is about a young black man with a tormented childhood and his struggle to overcome the consequences of his past with the help of a psychiatrist played by Denzel Washington, who also directed the project.

Another black film receiving good reviews was *The Great Debaters* (2007), starring Washington as the coach of a debate team at a tiny all-black Texas college that succeeds to the point where it can compete against Harvard. The film earned a Golden Globe nomination for Best Picture but was shut out of Academy Award nominations.

The Progress Question

As the decade passes, and more black actors, filmmakers, and critics gain a foothold in Hollywood, the question remains, How much progress has been made since the days when the old stereotypes ruled the screen? There is no clear answer partly because there is disagreement on what exactly constitutes progress. Is it measured by the extent to which films accurately represent black culture, or is it measured by the extent to which films are color-blind? Should the goal be movies about blacks or movies about people who happen to be black?

Two films of the era illustrate the debate. Spike Lee's *Bamboozled* (2000) is about a black television producer pressured into creating a blackface minstrel show, *Mantan*, a reference to Mantan Moreland, the bug-eyed buffoon of the 1930s. Black activists protest the show, and a radical group eventually kidnaps and kills one of its stars; the message seemingly being that black culture must prevail over stereotypes created to entertain whites.

The Pursuit of Happyness, in contrast, is the story of a homeless single father's relationship with his son as he tries to better both their lives. But this true story about a black man, starring a black actor, could just as easily be about a white man, starring a white actor.

Two Viewpoints

The "integrationist" viewpoint is summed up by Halle Berry, who said after winning her Oscar: "I hope this means that they won't see our color. I think that's what makes us so unique. I think that

Blacks debate the nature of their progress in Hollywood since the days of *The Birth of a Nation*. Pictured is a scene from Spike Lee's 2000 film *Bamboozled*, which contributed its own viewpoint.

maybe now we'll start to be judged on our merit and our work."[88] But critic Iverem disagrees: "Some of us do want our color seen, as well as our history and stories told from our perspective."[89]

Iverem and others maintain that the hard-won success of blacks in motion pictures is only part of the ongoing story. While there have been forty blacks nominated in the Academy Award acting categories, only one black director has been nominated for an Oscar, John Singleton for *Boyz 'n the Hood*. "Those concerned with blacks' representation in films say the dearth of black directors, producers, writers and behind-the-scenes workers is just as important [as the success of actors]," Rick Lyman writes in the *New York Times*. "And most troubling, they say, is the lack of black studio and network executives, who would have the power to help change the face of the industry."[90] Until that changes, the richness of black culture may not be fully revealed to the broad swath of mainstream America by the medium best suited to do so.

Notes

Chapter One: Silent Stereotypes

1. Donald Bogle, *Toms, Coons, Mulattoes, Mammies & Bucks*. New York: Continuum, 2006, pp. 5–9.

2. Thomas Cripps, *Slow Fade to Black*. New York: Oxford University Press, 1993, p. 29.

3. Bogle, *Toms, Coons, Mulattoes, Mammies & Bucks*, p. 10.

4. Quoted in Cripps, *Slow Fade to Black*, p. 52.

5. Quoted in Edward Mapp, *Blacks in American Films: Today and Yesterday*. Metuchen, NJ: Scarecrow, 1972, p. 19.

6. Quoted in Peter Noble, *The Negro in Films*. New York: Arno, 1970, p. 47.

7. Bogle, *Toms, Coons, Mulattoes, Mammies & Bucks*, p. 23.

8. Quoted in Noble, *The Negro in Films*, p. 44.

9. Bogle, *Toms, Coons, Mulattoes, Mammies & Bucks*, p. 24.

10. Quoted in Noble, *The Negro in Films*, p. 33.

Chapter Two: The "Race Movies"

11. Quoted in Noble, *The Negro in Films*, p. 46.

12. Quoted in Cripps, *Slow Fade to Black*, p. 73.

13. Quoted in Cripps, *Slow Fade to Black*, p. 75.

14. Quoted in Cripps, *Slow Fade to Black*, p. 76.

15. Quoted in Arnie Bernstein, *Hollywood on Lake Michigan: 100 Years of Chicago and the Movies*. Chicago: Lake Claremont, 1998, p. 46.

16. Quoted in Cripps, *Slow Fade to Black*, p. 84.

17. Cripps, *Slow Fade to Black*, p. 89.

18. Quoted in Cripps, *Slow Fade to Black*, p. 184.

19. *"The Homesteader,"* Chicago Defender, February 22, 1919, p. 13.

20. Quoted in Cripps, *Slow Fade to Black*, p. 184.

21. Bogle, *Toms, Coons, Mulattoes, Mammies & Bucks*, p. 114.

Chapter Three: Singers and Servants

22. Quoted in Cripps, *Slow Fade to Black*, p. 237.

23. Quoted in Cripps, *Slow Fade to Black*, p. 242.

24. Quoted in Noble, *The Negro in Films*, p. 51.

25. Bogle, *Toms, Coons, Mulattoes, Mammies & Bucks*, p. 36.

26. Quoted in Cripps, *Slow Fade to Black*, p. 268.

27. Noble, *The Negro in Films*, p. 84.

28. Quoted in Bogle, *Toms, Coons, Mulattoes, Mammies & Bucks*, p. 59.

29. Bogle, *Toms, Coons, Mulattoes, Mammies & Bucks*, p. 86.

30. Quoted in Cripps, *Slow Fade to Black*, p. 361.

31. Quoted in Cripps, *Slow Fade to Black*, p. 364.

32. Bogle, *Toms, Coons, Mulattoes, Mammies & Bucks*, p. 98.

33. Quoted in Cripps, *Slow Fade to Black*, p. 387.

Chapter Four: War and Aftermath

34. Quoted in Bogle, *Toms, Coons, Mulattoes, Mammies & Bucks*, p. 138.

35. Quoted in Thomas Cripps, *Making Movies Black*. New York: Oxford University Press, 1993, p. 43.

36. Cripps, *Making Movies Black*, p. 43.

37. Quoted in Cripps, *Making Movies Black*, p. 50.

38. Quoted in Cripps, *Making Movies Black*, p. 54.

39. Quoted in Cripps, *Making Movies Black*, p. 46.

40. Quoted in Bogle, *Toms, Coons, Mulattoes, Mammies & Bucks*, p. 100.

41. Quoted in Bogle, *Toms, Coons, Mulattoes, Mammies & Bucks*, p. 129.

42. Cripps, *Making Movies Black*, p. 85.

43. Cripps, *Making Movies Black*, p. 68.

44. Bosley Crowther, "'Bataan' Film of Heroic Defense of Peninsula Starring Robert Taylor, Robert Walker and Thomas Mitchell, at Capitol," *New York Times*, June 4, 1943. http://movies.nytimes.com/movie/review?res=9A0DE0DA1638E33BBC4C53DFB0668388659EDE.

45. Cripps, *Making Movies Black*, p. 75.

46. Quoted in Cripps, *Making Movies Black*, p. 178.

47. Quoted in Bogle, *Toms, Coons, Mulattoes, Mammies & Bucks*, p. 136.

48. Quoted in Cripps, *Making Movies Black*, p. 190.

49. Quoted in Cripps, *Making Movies Black*, p. 192.

50. Cripps, *Making Movies Black*, p. 220.

51. Quoted in Bogle, *Toms, Coons, Mulattoes, Mammies & Bucks*, p. 144.

52. Quoted in Bogle, *Toms, Coons, Mulattoes, Mammies & Bucks*, p. 155.

53. Quoted in Bogle, *Toms, Coons, Mulattoes, Mammies & Bucks*, p. 179.

Chapter Five: The Troubled Times

54. Cripps, *Making Movies Black*, p. 250.

55. Quoted in Bogle, *Toms, Coons, Mulattoes, Mammies & Bucks*, p. 172.

56. Bogle, *Toms, Coons, Mulattoes, Mammies & Bucks*, p. 181.

57. Quoted in Cripps, *Making Movies Black*, p. 283.

58. Cripps, *Making Movies Black*, p. 284.

59. Quoted in Bogle, *Toms, Coons, Mulattoes, Mammies & Bucks*, p. 198.

60. Bosley Crowther, "Poitier Meets the Cockneys: He Plays Teacher Who Wins Pupils Over," *New York Times*, June 15, 1967. http://movies.ny times.com/movie/review?_r=1&res =9E06E3DF103AE63ABC4D52DFB 066838C679EDE&oref=slogin.

61. Bosley Crowther, "'Guess Who's Coming to Dinner' Arrives: Tracy-Hepburn Picture Opens at 2 Theaters," *New York Times*, December 12, 1967. http://movies.nytimes. com/movie/review?res=9C03E6DE 1430E23BBC4A52DFB467838C 679EDE.

62. Clifford Mason, "Why Does White America Love Sidney Poitier So?" *New York Times*, September 10, 1967. www.nytimes.com/packages/html/ movies/bestpictures/heat-ar.html.

63. Bogle, *Toms, Coons, Mulattoes, Mammies & Bucks*, p. 220.

64. Bogle, *Toms, Coons, Mulattoes, Mammies & Bucks*, p. 195.

Chapter Six: Blaxploitation and Beyond

65. Quoted in George Alexander, *Why We Make Movies*. New York: Harlem Moon, 2003, p. 23.

66. Jesse Rhines, *Black Film/White Money*. New Brunswick, NJ: Rutgers University Press, 1996, p. 43.

67. Quoted in Bogle, *Toms, Coons, Mulattoes, Mammies & Bucks*, p. 235.

68. Quoted in Bogle, *Toms, Coons, Mulattoes, Mammies & Bucks*, p. 236.

69. Bogle, *Toms, Coons, Mulattoes, Mammies & Bucks*, p. 239.

70. Quoted in Rhines, *Black Film/White Money*, p. 42.

71. Bogle, *Toms, Coons, Mulattoes, Mammies & Bucks*, p. 258.

72. Bogle, *Toms, Coons, Mulattoes, Mammies & Bucks*, p. 259.

73. Charles Harpole, *History of the American Cinema*. New York: Scribner, 1990, p. 219.

Chapter Seven: Spike and His Friends

74. Roger Ebert, *"Do the Right Thing,"* *Chicago Sun-Times*, June 30, 1989. http://rogerebert.suntimes.com/apps/ pbcs.dll/article?AID=/19890630/ REVIEWS/906300301/1023.

75. Quoted in Esther Iverem, *We Gotta Have It*. New York: Thunder's Mouth, 2006, p. 387.

76. Quoted in Melvin Donaldson, *Black Directors in Hollywood*. Austin: University of Texas Press, 2003, p. 153.

77. Donaldson, *Black Directors in Hollywood*, p. 244.

78. Amy Taubin, "Come On In, the Mainstream's Fine," *Village Voice*, October 20–26, 1999. www.village

voice.com/film/9942,taubin,
9240,20.html.

79. Janet Maslin, "Looking to the Dead
for Mirth and Inspiration," *New York
Times*, July 13, 1990. http://movies.
nytimes.com/movie/review?_r=1&res
=9C0CE2DB1439F930A25754C0A9
66958260&oref=slogin.

80. Rita Kempley, *"What's Love Got to Do
with It?"* *Washington Post*, June 11,
1993. www.washingtonpost. com/
wp-srv/style/longterm/movies/ vid-
eos/whatslovegottodowithitrkem
pley_a0a391.htm.

81. Roger Ebert, *"Eve's Bayou,"* *Chicago
Sun-Times*, November 7, 1997. http://
rogerebert.suntimes.com/apps/pbcs.
dll/article?AID=/19971107/
REVIEWS/711070303/1023.

82. Bogle, *Toms, Coons, Mulattoes, Mammies & Bucks*, p. 391.

83. Bogle, *Toms, Coons, Mulattoes, Mammies & Bucks*, p. 433.

Epilogue: Into the New Century

84. Quoted in Scott Bowles, "Black
Actors' Breakthrough Year," *USA
Today*, February 6, 2005. www.usa
today.com/life/movies/news/2005-02-
-06-black-actors_x.htm.

85. Quoted in Bowles, "Black Actors'
Breakthrough Year."

86. Quoted in David Germain, "Films
from 'Tsotsi' to 'Catch a Fire' Delve
Deep into the Heart of Africa and
Audiences Are Enjoying the Journey,"
Newsday, November 5, 2006.
www.newsday.com/entertain
ment/movies/ny-ffmov4956137
nov05,0,7551808.story?coll=ny-
moviereview-headlines.

87. Iverem, *We Gotta Have It*, p. 219.

88. Quoted in David Germain, "Halle
Berry, Denzel Washington Make
Oscars History," *Christian Science
Monitor*, March 24, 2002. www.cs
monitor.com/specials/oscars02.

89. Iverem, *We Gotta Have It*, p. 345.

90. Rick Lyman, "Black Actors: Still
Keeping Their Eyes on the Prize,"
New York Times, February 27, 2002.
http://query.nytimes.com/gst/full
page.html?res=9D0DE4DA1731F9
34A15751C0A9649C8B63.

Chronology

1903
White actors in blackface appear in the first film version of *Uncle Tom's Cabin.*

1912
The first all-black film, *The Pullman Porter*, is released.

1914
Sam Lucas becomes the first black actor in a major role in *Uncle Tom's Cabin.*

1915
Black leaders protest negative racial stereotypes in *The Birth of a Nation.*

1916
George and Noble Johnson form the all-black Lincoln Motion Picture Company.

1919
Oscar Micheaux's first film, *The Homesteader*, premiers in Chicago.

1927
The first major sound film, *The Jazz Singer*, is released.

1929
The first all-black musical films, *Hearts in Dixie* and *Hallelujah!*, are released.

1940
Hattie McDaniel wins the Best Supporting Actress Academy Award for *Gone with the Wind* (1939).

1942
NAACP executive secretary Walter White issues a statement on the depiction of blacks in motion pictures.

1955
Dorothy Dandridge is nominated for the Best Actress Academy Award for *Carmen Jones* (1954).

1964
Sidney Poitier wins the Best Actor Academy Award for *Lilies in the Field* (1963).

1971
The "blaxploitation" era begins with *Sweet Sweetback's Baadasssss Song.*

1986
Three black actresses—Whoopi Goldberg, Margaret Avery, and Oprah Winfrey—receive Academy Award nominations for *The Color Purple* (1985).

1992
John Singleton becomes the first black director nominated for an Academy Award, for *Boyz 'n the Hood* (1991).

2002
Black artists win both Best Actor (Denzel Washington, *Training Day* [2001]) and Best Actress (Halle Berry, *Monster's Ball* [2001]) Academy Awards.

For More Information

Books

Carol Bergman, *Sidney Poitier*. Black American Series. New York: Chelsea House, 1988. This simply written biography traces Poitier's journey from poverty-stricken youth to Academy Award–winning actor. Includes an introduction by Coretta Scott King.

James Earl Hardy, *Spike Lee*. Black Americans of Achievement Series. New York: Chelsea House, 1996. Account of the filmmaker's family life and unique approach to movies about racial issues. Includes photographs from some of Lee's movies.

Cookie Lommel, *Black Filmmakers*. African American Achievers Series. Philadelphia: Chelsea House, 2002. A survey of the history of black film and the careers of such artists as Sidney Poitier, Denzel Washington, Lena Horne, and Spike Lee.

George Nelson, *Blackface: Reflections on African-Americans and the Movies*. New York: HarperCollins, 1994. A lively history of black films that pays special attention to those made since 1980.

Berry S. Torriano, *The 50 Most Influential Black Films*. New York: Citadel, 2002. The author's selections are grouped according to decade, starting with *The Pullman Porter* in 1912 and ending with *The Best Man* in 1999.

Internet Sources

African Americans in Motion Pictures: The Past and the Present. B. Davis Schwartz Memorial Library, Long Island University, C.W. Post Campus. (www.liu.edu/cwis/cwp/library/african/movies.htm). Loaded with information, including film history, short biographies, lists of top black films.

Black Film Center/Archive, Indiana University, Department of African-American and African Diaspora Studies. (www.indiana.edu/~bfca/index.html). Web site of an academic center that collects black films. Especially interesting are short clips showing blacks in films prior to 1900.

Blackflix.com: African-American Movie Stars, Reviews, Interviews and More. (www.blackflix.com/index.shtml). Has some historical material but is mostly devoted to recent and future black films and performers.

Blaxploitation.com: A Soulful Tribute. (www.blaxploitation.com). Articles on and pictures from the explosion of violence-based black films in the early 1970s.

Midnight Ramble. (www.moderntimes. com/palace/black). Good material on blacks in the early decades of motion pictures, including plenty of photographs of performers from "Sunshine Sammy" to Lena Horne.

Video Media

Small Steps, Big Strides: The Black Experience in Hollywood. Image Entertainment, 1998. Narrated by Louis Gossett Jr., this video features rare film clips and behind-the-scenes looks at black film through the decades.

That's Black Entertainment: A Three Part Original Documentary Series Celebrating Black Actors, Comedians, and Westerns. S'more Entertainment, 2006. Documentary on the black film industry of the 1920s, 1930s, and 1940s.

Midnight Ramble: The Story of the Black Film Industry. Shanachie Video, 1995. Examination of the black "race movies" from 1910 through the 1940s with special attention to Oscar Micheaux.

Index

Picture Credits

Cover: AP Images
AP Images, 26, 88
© Bettmann/Corbis, 47
CBS Photo Archive via Getty Images, 20
Columbia Tristar/Getty Images, 62
© Content Mine International/Alamy, 80, 84
© Corbis, 14
Epic/The Kobal Collection, 15
40 Acres & A Mule/New Line/The Kobal Collection, 92
Hulton Archive/Getty Images, 11
© John Springer Collection/Corbis, 40
© JP Laffont/Sygma/Corbis, 66

MGM/Photofest, Inc., 38
© Michael Ochs Archives/Corbis, 22
Micheaux Film Corp./Photofest, Inc., 28
Paramount/The Kobal Collection, 73
Photofest, Inc., 9
Pictorial Parade/Getty Images, 34
20th Century Fox/The Kobal Collection, 64, 71
20th Century Fox/Photofest, Inc., 31, 55
© Underwood & Underwood/Corbis, 58
United Artists/The Kobal Collection, 57
Universal/The Kobal Collection, 78
Walt Disney/The Kobal Collection, 50
Warner Bros./The Kobal Collection, 74

About the Author

William W. Lace is a native of Fort Worth, Texas, where he is executive assistant to the chancellor at Tarrant County College. He holds a bachelor's degree from Texas Christian University, a master's degree from East Texas State University, and a doctorate from the University of North Texas. Prior to joining Tarrant County College, he was director of the News Service at the University of Texas at Arlington and a sportswriter and columnist for the *Fort Worth Star-Telegram*. He has written more than forty-five nonfiction books for young readers on subjects ranging from the atomic bomb to the Dallas Cowboys. He and his wife, Laura, a retired school librarian, live in Arlington, Texas, and have two children and four grandchildren.